CREATED FOR HAPPINESS
Understanding Your Life in God

Cynthia A. Bond Hopson and
Sarah Heaner Lancaster
Participant's Guide by Cynthia A. Bond Hopson

United
Methodist
Women
FAITH · HOPE · LOVE IN ACTION

ISBN: 978-1-940182-21-6
Library of Congress Control Number: 2014955770

Cover design: René Ríos
Cover image: ©deviantArt by Olivia Michalski

Printed in the United States of America

United Methodist Women PURPOSE

The organized unit of United Methodist Women shall be a community of women whose purpose is to know God and to experience freedom as whole persons through Jesus Christ; to develop a creative, supportive fellowship; and to expand concepts of mission through participation in the global ministries of the church.

The Vision

Turning faith, hope and love into action on behalf of women, children and youth around the world.

Living the Vision

We provide opportunities and resources to grow spiritually, become more deeply rooted in Christ and put faith into action.

We are organized for growth, with flexible structures leading to effective witness and action.

We equip women and girls around the world to be leaders in communities, agencies, workplaces, governments and churches.

We work for justice through compassionate service and advocacy to change unfair policies and systems.

We provide educational experiences that lead to personal change in order to transform the world.

Contents

Introduction

"Develop the happiness habit . . . "[1] It sounds easy enough, most of us want to be happy, and we're darned happy to pay for a chance to make happiness habit-forming. Despite the adage that money can't buy happiness, a bunch of us are trying to purchase a reasonable facsimile—every year Americans spend billions for self-help and personal products to improve their lives and lot in life.

People want to be happy. Nothing could be more obvious, and yet this common and evident goal is not as easy to achieve as it is to desire. The things we think will make us happy do not always do so. We know we want to be happy. We may even think that we ought to be happy, believing that something is wrong if we do not feel good. Almost everyone has some period in her or his life when happiness is difficult. For some, that period may be relatively short, but for others it may continue for years. Realizing the vast gap between the happiness we want and what we actually feel can make us even more unhappy. On the other hand, when life is going well and we feel satisfied, we may take happiness for granted—perhaps even believing we have a right to have it (and not just the right to pursue it). No matter what the case may be, the concept of happiness has a central place in human life.

We live in a time when the search for happiness has become a dominant topic in our culture. Any perfunctory Internet search for happiness and related topics will yield more results—today's count: thirty-two million—than any human could possibly read or absorb. They tout everything from happiness reminders, quotes, sayings, stories, memories, and songs to special-order pencils about this difficult to describe and define emotional state of being. People share techniques for being happy in magazines, books, and websites that come from psychology, philosophy, and even other religions.

According to Psychologist Ed Diener, happiness is subjective and is "a combination of life satisfaction and having more positive emotions than negative."[2] Simply put, we want to be happy and, if possible, we want to be happy now or at least on the path that leads us there. Most of us would probably agree that we're either happy or not, and indeed we do know it, as the folk song "If You're Happy and You Know It" says.

John Powell's book, "Happiness Is an Inside Job," explains that "by practicing ten life tasks outlined by this popular spiritual leader,"[3] readers can get to work and find the happiness they seek. Though the author doesn't make this job simplistic or beat the Pollyanna drum, we are led to believe that happiness may be just a few short steps or clicks away. Yet evidence from around the world suggests that happiness comes from within and it comes in all shapes and sizes.

One thing we do know for sure: "stuff" doesn't bring or make happiness. In an unscientific survey conducted for this study, participants were asked what makes them happy. The replies ranged from more money, no bills or worries about paying for children's college, good health, and access to funds to travel to all the places on her or his bucket list.

Sadly, lottery winners and others who instantaneously come into large chunks of money soon learn that their problems didn't go away when they had more "stuff." They may not have had the same problems as before, but there was still something else blocking their full access to complete happiness. First, they had to learn the difference between being rich (self-centered and lavishing all their resources on themselves) and wealthy (gaining satisfaction through philanthropic deeds).

Secondly, many lottery winners soon discover that they have many "lost" relatives who have fallen on hard times and need a loan. Or, illness strikes and the prognosis is bleak. Finally, poor financial management and lavish lifestyles often lands these families in worse shape than they were before the windfall.

So, in this lifelong pursuit of happiness, what, pray tell, are we looking for? Is it an elusive hunt destined to drive us to madness, or is it the poignant realization that we, like the Apostle Paul, can be content no matter what our circumstances are?[4] If we spend too much time searching, obsessing, and pursuing happiness, we may indeed be "standing knee-deep in a river and dying of thirst" as country singer Kathy Mattea said in her powerful 1992 hit.[5]

The search for happiness in our time is widespread, and it draws from many sources of wisdom. However, a specifically Christian viewpoint has been largely absent from this cultural conversation. We know that Christians have good news to share about salvation. Do we have any good news to share about happiness?

It may seem odd to think of happiness as important in Christian life. For many years now, it has been common for Christians to think of happiness as an unimportant goal, reserving the word "joy" for the true satisfaction of Christian life. This distinction between happiness (pleasant but temporary earthly feelings) and joy (lasting contentment in relationship with God), though, is a fairly recent development. For centuries, Christians did not see happiness as less than joy. Notable theologians such as Augustine and Thomas Aquinas shared their views on happiness. Augustine is well known for having said that we are restless until we rest in God, and resting in God's blessed life brings us true happiness. Thomas Aquinas pointed out that the things (like wealth and power) that we think will bring happiness do not. He knew that the only happiness that would not disappoint us was happiness in God. Christians did make a distinction between true and false happiness (just as they did between true and false joy) but the word "happiness" was perfectly acceptable for describing Christian life. By abandoning the word "happiness," Christians cut themselves off from resources in the tradition that could still inform us about happiness. We also make it seem that a basic human value has nothing to do with the Christian faith, but nothing could be further from the truth.

Furthermore, by refusing to use the word, we have handed it over to secular culture, letting bars with "happy hours" or advertising agencies define happiness. Because advertisers want us to buy the products they are advertising, they present those products as if the consumers of those products are happy. The implication is that happiness comes from being able to consume what we desire, rather than from the process of self-transformation that religious life makes possible.[6] Christians, and particularly Methodists, have much to say about this topic that is different from what secular culture has to say. We have good news to share about what real happiness is, and we should not keep it all to ourselves.

The early Methodist tradition used the language of happiness often. John Wesley preached about happiness almost as often as he preached about holiness. Indeed, for him, happiness and holiness were together the goal of Christian life. He had much to say about what genuine happiness ought to be, and when it was understood properly, happiness and salvation belonged together.

Wesley could hold these together so closely because he understood salvation to be about more than what happens to us after we die. Salvation is also about living this life the way that God created it to be lived. Because he understood salvation to matter now, and not just after death, he saw that it was integrally connected to our happiness. He learned from the great theologians who came before him that humans are most happy when they fulfill the purpose that God has given to all of us, namely to reflect the image of God in the way we live.

Embracing a long tradition about how to read Genesis 1:26–27, Wesley understood that humans were made for happiness. He did not mean that humans were made to have fun or to be in a good mood all the time. We were made to be happy in God, to know and love God in such a deep and powerful way that the relationship fulfills us and makes us whole. This is true, because having been made in the image of God, we are most truly ourselves when we reflect the love of God in all that we do. Our task in this life after the fall, which damaged the image of God in us, is for that image to be healed so that we love as God loves—at least as nearly as it is possible for a human to do. Having this image of God renewed in us is the essence of salvation. Wesley called it "the one thing needful." Everything about one's life as a Christian ought to lead to that goal. The way of salvation that he preached was intended to show us how to be restored to the happiness and holiness for which we were made. For Wesley, then, the way of salvation was also the way of happiness.

So, Wesley did not think of happiness as simply having a life full of pleasant experiences, but he did think that as we made progress along the way of salvation, we learned how to enjoy the world as God would have us enjoy it. Being happy in God includes taking pleasure in the world that God created, but Wesley was careful to say that such pleasure should never displace God. It was right relationship with God that allowed us to value God's creation as God values it, and so to delight in it appropriately.

Not only did John Wesley preach and teach about happiness, but his brother Charles also wrote hymns about happiness that the early Methodists sang. The Wesleys and the early Methodists could focus so much on happiness because they understood it to be biblical to do so. The happiness they sought was happiness in God, and so the happiness they found was the most secure and fulfilling possible. This study will examine the understanding of happiness that they held and how they learned to live the life that God called them to.

Come, let us be intentionally prayerful, patient, and persistent as we explore and discover how God's grace and love offers peace, contentment, joy, and that something very special we know as "happiness" to all those who seek richer meaning.

ENDNOTES

1. John Powell, *Happiness Is an Inside Job*, rev. ed. (East Lansing, Mich: Tabor Publishing, 1989), publisher summary.

2. "What is happiness?" *This Emotional Life*, PBS, 2011, www.pbs.org/thisemotionallife/topic/happiness/what-happiness.

3. Powell, *Happiness Is an Inside Job*, publisher summary.

4. Phillipians 4:11

5. Kathy Mattea, "Standing Knee Deep in a River (Dying of Thirst)," *Lonesome Standard Time*, 1992.

6. Vincent J. Miller, *Consuming Religion: Christian Faith and Practice in a Consumer Culture*, (New York: Continuum, 2004), 144.

CHAPTER 1

Defining Happiness

By Cynthia A. Bond Hopson

Happiness is big business, and that's no laughing matter. An Internet search using Google revealed that in 2008 alone, more than $11 billion was spent on self-improvement books, CDs, seminars, coaching, and stress management programs.[1] Further, if you do an Internet search of the word "happiness," you get everything from how and what to do to live happily, definitions, happiness quotes and lessons, and how to deliver happiness. A sobering statement from TIME.com that turned up in one of these searches explains that, "Americans are free to pursue happiness, but there's no guarantee they will achieve it. The secret is knowing how and where to look."[2]

Some articles outline the ten things you need to do to be happier, while others suggest that singing in the choir or doing other tasks can make you happy. At the heart of all this warm fuzziness is a fluid motion—something that gets prompted by an action and then a reaction, something highly sought after and craved, but often elusive and fleeting.

So, then we are left to imagine that whoever wrote that ditty about being happy and knowing it was obviously singing in the choir or had read the book about what it takes to be happy, even though defining happiness is much like Supreme Court Justice Potter Stewart's infamous statement about pornography: "We can't define it but we know it when we see it!"[3]

Have you ever used the terms happiness, joy, contentment, and self-improve-ment interchangeably to describe your or someone else's current state? We clap most times at the beginning of this familiar "If you're happy . . . " tune because we are happy people and it is a tune that evokes good memories. The instructions are so simple that anybody can follow them—happy or not—but how do you know you're really happy? Is it a feeling, a state of mind, or a trait that only some people possess? Is it really contagious as motivational speakers tell us? Must we expect more meaningful feelings for confirmation that we're truly happy and joyful?

It is hard to define happiness without using the word "happy." If you ask ten people to define it, you will probably get ten different but similar responses. Diener's definition used in the Introduction isn't concrete perhaps because it is difficult to define happiness without using the word happy.

And we have to decide if we're talking about regular old happiness or "true" happiness, which provides a completely different set of results in an Internet search engine. My search results included this quote from Indian philosopher and activist Mahatma Gandhi: "Happiness is when what you think, what you say and what you do are in harmony."[4] My results also included one from John W. Gardner, educator, leader, and activist, that describes true happiness as the full use of one's power and talents.[5]

Authors Rick Foster and Greg Hicks define happiness as a profound, endur-ing feeling of contentment, capability, and centeredness. They write that a rich sense of well-being comes from knowing that you can deal productively and creatively with all that life offers—the good and the bad—and that the source of happiness is to be found in the way you choose to live your life. They describe nine choices extremely happy people share and these include being intentional, being open to life's options, and being accountable for one's own actions.[6]

Dictionary.com describes happiness as "the quality or state of being happy." The second definition describes it as "good fortune; pleasure; contentment;

joy."[7] The entry includes a list of synonyms like "pleasure, joy, exhilaration, bliss, contentedness, delight, enjoyment and satisfaction"[8]—words we often use interchangeably to describe our happy moments and situations.

Popular author and speaker Nell W. Mohney, who writes extensively on spiritual disciplines and joyous living, explains that, "the basic answer to happiness is a spiritual one."[9] She enthusiastically advocates for gratitude as an "antidote for worry, stress, depression, and grief," all those things that can rob us of many of the good emotions mentioned above.[10]

Happiness is "a feeling . . . a state of mind when you feel very special and calm," according to Ask.com.[11] Interestingly, this imprecise and abstract definition immediately paints a picture for me of a hammock strung between two shady oak trees, a great novel to read between dozes, some chilled lemonade, a gentle breeze. Yep, that seems to be happiness, but is that all there is? And how do we get to this "happy" place?

Aristotle, the Greek philosopher, said centuries ago that happiness is not measured with money or goods, but through balancing reasons and desires with moderation. What a novel idea!

According to the information we have thus far, we can agree that happiness is (1) a feeling that comes over you when life is good; (2) the opposite of sadness;[12] (3) something we can show and describe better than we can define; (4) a "phenomenon that is difficult to measure and is thus best experienced by each individual;"[13] (5) "a true state of mind that you can have anytime, anywhere. It comes from love, wholeness and peace. It is an inner state of being that comes naturally as you become connected with who you really are, your gifts and your purpose."[14]

Unpacking the definitions of happiness yields a list of attributes for us to examine more fully. Happiness is:

- A natural feeling prompted by a good life.
- Connectedness to love, inner peace, and wholeness.

- The opposite of sad.
- Important, but hard to grasp and often fleeting.
- Available anytime, anywhere, but only after you discover your talents and purpose.

Salesman John Parker of Nashville, Tennessee, is a unique blend of joy and happiness and could be a poster child for all the above. Here are his words on the topic:

> I'm out there making people smile. I'm happy. People make me smile, I make them smile. Pass it on. That's joy! That's where I get my joy from—seeing people happy. I hate seeing people down and everything. Sometimes you have to be, sometimes I am, but I try to hide mine.[15]

Parker is a vendor for *The Contributor*, a two dollar newspaper "offering diverse perspectives on homelessness and providing genuine opportunities for advancement"[16] to those who are homeless and formerly homeless. He is waiting for settlement of a disability claim so he can afford somewhere nice to live—in the meantime, he's staying at the Nashville Rescue Mission and having a ball with his regular customers and the children who look for him on their favorite corner.

He's absolutely basking in a natural feeling, using his talents, knows his purpose, is connected to love, has inner peace, and is on his way to wholeness. Perhaps John Parker is a gentle reminder that everything doesn't have to be picture-perfect for happiness to occur—he does sing in the choir and said his ultimate goal is getting closer to God. He plans to teach his children to do the same because he says, "without God, I wouldn't be nothin'."[17]

Wayne Sampe, also a *Contributor* vendor, echoes this same philosophy and attitude about being happy:

My momma said "You're gonna live until you die, and you might as well die with a smile on your face instead of a frown." Why worry about something you ain't got no control over? . . . I put it in God's hands.[18]

Human relations guru Dale Carnegie also discovered these truths long ago and discussed them in his booklet *The Little Recognized Secret of Success*, first published in 1965. Whether through his parents' lessons or by trial and error, he stated emphatically that neither money nor fame ensures happiness. "Happiness depends primarily (in addition to good health) on one thing only: your thoughts. If we can do that, we will be on the high road to solving all our problems,"[19] Carnegie said.

Is it possible to be too happy?

About five years ago, Gayle (not her real name) read that happiness was a choice, so she "chose" to be happy and she decided to seize every possible opportunity to wallow in it. She started using the question, "Which will I regret more—doing it or not doing it?" as her measuring stick for action.

When her favorite sister turned fifty, she opted to skip a distant relative's funeral and attend the birthday party. Instead of sitting in the second tier of a Broadway theater like she had done on her first visit to New York City, she bought the best seat available and saw *Driving Miss Daisy* in the third row from the front.

She made conscious decisions to: (1) tie sadness up tightly and keep his little ugly butt in the corner; (2) keep negativity in all its forms—people, places, and things—as far away as possible, and (3) begin prioritizing the things she really wanted to do.

This year she's been to her fortieth anniversary high school reunion, a family gathering, a family reunion (to different events), her best friend's graduation from college, and she saw two more Broadway shows.

Today, she describes herself as "happier than I know how to be—giddy even! This can't last!"[20] Though she doesn't mean to, she's waiting for the proverbial "other shoe to drop,"[21] and mentally preparing for the inevitable heartache or phone call that might come and completely change her life and circumstances. The questions are, then, how long can/should we plan to live in this elevated state of happiness, and is it the opposite of living in fear? Many of us have never faced our fears or allowed ourselves to be happy—we don't try anything new because we're afraid we might fail.

We may be suffering from childhood wounds and have a difficult time believing we're worthy of happiness. If you've recently lost a spouse, child, parent, or someone close to you, you may be in such a deep, dark place that happiness is a foreign concept, yet these are the times when God loves you most. When Thomas Moore wrote the immortal words to the sacred hymn, "Come, Ye Disconsolate" almost two hundred years ago, he heard God saying "Here bring your wounded hearts, here tell your anguish; Earth has no sorrow that heaven cannot heal. Joy of the desolate, . . . hope of the penitent, fadeless and pure!"[22]

These lyrics have never been more important for us to hear and bask in than they are today, especially as we grapple with and pursue happiness. Moore was inspired by God's infinite love as expressed in Jeremiah 31:3, "I have loved you with an everlasting love; therefore I have continued my faithfulness to you."

We might as well relax and work, like John Parker, toward a closer relationship with God, because as the saying goes: "When the going gets tough, the tough get going and the weak drop out."

"I'VE GOT THAT JOY, JOY, JOY, JOY DOWN IN MY HEART"

Joy, contentment, peace, and happiness are often used interchangeably, and while they may be considered synonyms, as mentioned earlier, one is often used in defining the other. *Merriam-Webster's Eleventh Collegiate Dictionary* describes joy as "The emotion evoked by well-being, success or good fortune or the prospect of possessing what one desires."[23] (By permission. From *Merriam-Webster's Collegiate® Dictionary*, 11th edition, ©2014 by Merriam-Webster, Inc., www.merriam-webster.com.) The entry for joy has a much broader description of what the emotion looks like and how to know if you have it, while happiness is simply defined as "a state of contentment."[24] What their definitions have in common is satisfaction and emotion prompted by a state of being, and an acknowledgement that one is an extension of the other. Both are heart-related and reflect a current frame of mind—it is difficult to be in a state of satisfaction and contentment if your heart is troubled, whether from external toil and turmoil or from less-than-ideal emotions raging inside. Chapters 4–7 will seek to describe happiness in detail from biblical and theological perspectives.

Listen to the words of James 1:2–4 and ponder his understanding of the concept of joy: ". . . whenever you face trials of any kind, consider it nothing but joy, because you know that the testing of your faith produces endurance; and let endurance have its full effect, so that you may be mature and complete, lacking in nothing." *The Living Bible* says, "Dear brothers, is your life full of difficulties and temptations? Then be happy . . ."

James seems to say even when you are not joyful or happy, you can still count it as such. He espouses that when your trials and tribulations come, as they often will, they are tests to help you mature and grow, so endure and rejoice through it all. In Chapter 4, we will see that the Bible teaches us that happiness is based on our relationship with Jesus Christ.

I SAW A HAPPY PERSON ONCE AND SHE . . .

One thing is for sure—happy people are a joy to be around and are always a welcome addition to any gathering. They smile, they make others smile, and when all is said and done, we feel 100 percent better after basking in their presence. They literally brighten the corners where they are.

Not surprisingly, happy people have attributes in common, and while these can't be bottled up, duplicated, or cloned (at least not yet), happy people inspire us and remind us to model the life of Jesus Christ. They scatter joy and happiness like raindrops on an April afternoon. Like John Parker and Wayne Sampe, thinking of them makes us smile, and when they share their brand of happiness, we absolutely know we have been in the presence of God.

If we asked you to list the ten happiest people you know, chances are at least three or four people would immediately come to mind. The other four or five might take a little more thought. The late tennis great Arthur Ashe and Carnegie Mellon Professor Randy Pausch belong on any list of happiness heroes we might assemble. Through their service to humankind and sacrificial living, they shared their days of grace with us.

Ashe was the first African-American male to win three Grand Slam titles in tennis, a sport in which he was the "first and only" for many years after he made his professional debut in 1970. He won the U.S. Open in 1968 while he was still an amateur, and remains the only African-American male to win Wimbledon, the U.S. Open, and to be ranked number one in the world. He grew up during the era of segregation in Richmond, Virginia, and his mother's death while he was young threw his life into a tailspin. As a young man, he experienced racism and hard times first-hand, but his father encouraged him and kept a tight rein on Ashe to keep him out of trouble.

After contracting AIDS through a blood transfusion during heart surgery, Ashe became a vocal advocate for critical research and enhanced education about the disease, its causes, and treatment. Before his untimely death in 1993, he started a foundation and laid the groundwork for a $5 million fundraising campaign. He was awarded the Presidential Medal of Freedom, the United States of America's highest civilian honor. Always the activist, he was arrested at one of his last public appearances at a Washington, D.C., protest against the treatment of Haitian refugees.

He gently reminded us in an oft-repeated quote that, "True heroism is remarkably sober, very undramatic. It is not the urge to surpass all others at whatever cost, but the urge to serve others at whatever cost."[25]

Professor Pausch came into the public eye in 2007, shortly before his death from pancreatic cancer at age forty-seven. Pausch's matter-of-fact approach to his impending death inspired students and strangers alike with his hopes for a world of peace and dreams fulfilled. His "Last Lecture: Really Achieving Your Childhood Dreams" was part of an ongoing lecture series called "Journeys," in which top academics were asked to think deeply about what matters to them and share a hypothetical final talk.

He shared his hopes of playing in the National Football League, and what he learned because that dream didn't come true. An official Star Trek fan, he made a cameo appearance in a scene from the movie. As a final act of heroism and humility, he donated the $217.06 paycheck he received from the movie appearance to charity.[26]

Happy people tend to naturally serve others and possess a set of traits that are fairly easy to define and list:

- Living in community;
- Taking risks;
- Living fearlessly and taking each day as it comes;
- Mentoring and sharing what they know and have;
- Living and giving generously and benevolently to others;
- Challenging themselves daily to live beyond expectations;
- Befriending and learning from children and the elderly;
- Learning to balance what is important to them with what matters;
- Becoming richer through their relationship to the arts, music, and books;
- Knowing and understanding the power of laughter—they laugh at themselves and with us;
- Exercising, resting, and refreshing themselves so they can shine brightly;
- Looking at the world through a positive lens;

- Learning from their mistakes and teaching the lessons to others;
- Holding themselves and others to high standards and accountability;
- Making others "taller not smaller"[27] when they leave their presence;
- Offering and maintaining a non-anxious presence for mediation and peacemaking to avoid confusion and confrontation;
- Maintaining their full presence for conversations and not getting co-opted by distractions;
- Finding work they can be passionate about; and
- Respecting the past for its rich memories without living in it.

FROM THE RAT RACE AND BUMPER CARS TO CARPOOLING

"Would you walk with the Lord, in the light of His word, and have peace and contentment alway? You must do His sweet will to be free from all ill . . . "[28]

Most of us think we know contentment when we see it, yet very few people describe themselves as contented without being prompted by a predetermined list of possibilities. Do we know how to be contented—described as "feeling or showing satisfaction with one's possessions, status, or situation?"[29] Plainly stated, it suggests that we are satisfied with where we are at this time in our lives. We are where we want to be, we have what we need, and nothing more is needed, desired, or solicited. We are enjoying the perfect gooey sundae with lots of everything we love on it. We are relaxing in the porch swing after a long walk down a winding road complete with a meandering stream of clear, cool water and the smell of honeysuckle. We have just helped Habitat for Humanity build its one-hundreth home for a mother and two young daughters, Faith and Hope. It really doesn't get any better than this.

Elisha Hoffman's classic hymn, "Is Your All on the Altar?" describes peace and contentment as walking with the Lord "in the light of His word" and indicates that surrendering to God is the only way to contentment. The opening stanza talks about longing for "sweet peace and for faith to increase,"[30] but still surmises that our efforts are futile and unproductive until we surrender our "all," meaning our hopes, dreams, talents, will, and intentions to God for safekeeping.

Contentment seems to be a journey—one doesn't just wake up one morning and decide to be content. It is a process arrived at through trial and error, reflection, contemplation, longing, and acceptance. The popular online *Urban Dictionary* describes it as "true peace of mind that doesn't have anything to do with any external pleasure or condition, but rather your attitude. There is no natural limit to desiring things. You will go on desiring more and more your whole life until you unconsciously decide it's good enough."[31]

Finding happiness and contentment often comes after major life events—marriage, childbirth, job loss, completion of educational requirements—and a sincere re-evaluation of all that encompasses what we call "our lives." *Simple Abundance: A Daybook of Comfort and Joy* by Sarah Ban Breathnach is a collection of 366 essays for "women who wish to live by their own lights." In this book she invites readers to "embrace the book's gentle lessons, savor its sublime common sense, dare to live its passionate truth, and share its extraordinary and exhilarating gift with every woman"[32] they encounter.

Simple Abundance shows women how to make their daily lives an expression of their authentic selves by joining spirituality with lifestyle. Margaret Young's words in the Foreword ties a tidy knot in our quest for meaning. Young says people often work harder to get more material things and trappings, thinking they will make them happier. She explains, "The way it actually works is the reverse. You must first be who you really are, then do what you need to do, in order to have what you want."[33] Ban Breathnach seems to be a perfect example of this. She said she wrote *Simple Abundance* to "reconcile her deepest spiritual, authentic and creative longings with often overwhelming and conflicting commitments to her family and other entities.[34]

She describes herself as "a workaholic, careaholic, and perfectionist"[35] and she suspected she was not the only one out there. She was right. More than seven million copies of the book have been sold and it still remains popular. Chapter 7 of this study also examines the biblical link between simplicity and happiness.

HAPPINESS MAY BE AFFECTED BY LIFE CIRCUMSTANCES

The carpool lane is an often-unexpected place that people find themselves, but many discover becoming a Christian and/or a parent shifts priorities and often brings with it a re-evaluation of what is important.

When another heir to the British throne, George Alexander Louis, was born in July 2013, his father, Prince William, remarked that a new sense of responsibility had descended upon him with fatherhood. "Something I never thought I would feel myself . . . a lot of things affect me differently now."[36]

Actresses Jennifer Garner and Brooke Burke-Charvet regularly carpool as part of their mommy duties. More and more celebrities are refusing roles that keep them away from their families and their children's routines. Country music super-couple Tim McGraw and Faith Hill head to Las Vegas on weekends to do their shows so as not to interfere with their three teenaged daughters' schedules. McGraw, who also acts, plans to do other films when the timing will permit.

Lynn (not her real name) said her high-powered government job had changed her into someone she didn't recognize. She discussed this with her husband, Clyde, and they began a discernment process as they prayed, along with making their New Year's resolutions.

When her program's funding was not renewed, she leapt at the opportunity to be a stay-at-home mother to her children, Mindy, three, and Zachariah, seven. She said dropping Zach off at school and being home to greet him at the end of the day is a real treat for both of them. The benefits of leaving her job and staying home made getting out of the rat race so much easier. She is content to work from home to supplement their income but has no plans to seek outside employment.

Peace is part of those things that make for happiness. Peace is often conceived of as absence of war or turmoil. However, peace, allied to happiness, is more than that. It is a living, growing network of relationships called *"shalom"* in the Bible. Shalom embodies positive peace. It is harmony, well-being, wholeness, and positive relationship with God, fellow humans, community, and creation. Shalom is closely related to justice, as it is described in Isaiah 32:16–18.

Peace is reconciling differences and embarking on a path for renewed growth and coherence. Peace will take us on a journey, an inward path of introspection offered by God that "surpasses all understanding" (Philippians 4:7) and can lead to an outcome of right relationships, both personally and collectively.

Chapter 7 links happiness to an understanding that we must first be true to God to discover and receive happiness rather than seeking it in secular realms.

ENDNOTES

1. Melanie Lindner, "What People Are Still Willing to Pay For," *Forbes*, January 5, 2009, www.forbes.com/2009/01/15/self-help-industry-ent-sales-cx_ml_0115selfhelp.html.

2. Jeffrey Kluger, "The Happiness of Pursuit," *Time*, July 8, 2013, http://content.time.com/time/magazine/article/0,9171,2146449,00.html.

3. Jacobellis v. Ohio, 378 US 184 (1964).

4. Mahatma Gandhi, as quoted in "Discover True Happiness," MyVisions_MyIdeals, March 6, 2011, http://myvisionsmyideals.blogspot.com/2011/03/discover-true-happiness.html.

5. John W. Gardner, as quoted on World Best Seminars: Success Inspirational Quotes, November 2013, http://worldbestseminars.comtrue-happiness-involves-the-full-use-of-ones-power-and-talents-john-w-gardner.

6. Rick Foster and Greg Hicks, *How We Choose to Be Happy: The 9 Choices of Extremely Happy People—Their Secrets, Their Stories* (New York: G.P. Putnam's Sons, 1999), 2.

7. happiness. Dictionary.com. *Dictionary.com Unabridged*. Random House, Inc. http://dictionary.reference.com/browse/happiness (accessed: September 22, 2014).

8. Ibid.

9. Nell W. Mohney, *Just Choose Happiness: A Guide to Joyous Living*, (Nashville: Abingdon Press, 2009), vii.

10. Ibid., 11.

11. "What is happiness?" 2014, www.ask.com/web-answers/Society/Philosophy/what_is_happiness.

12. "Happiness," 2014, www.vocabulary.com/dictionary/happiness.

13. Joseph Amagada, "Definition of Happiness—What Is Happiness?" Ezine Articles, March 1, 2009, http://ezinearticles.com/?Definition-of-Happiness—What-is-Happiness?&id=2050358.

14. Ibid.

15. John Parker, *The Contributor*, www.thecontributor.org, August 1–14, 2013, 3.

16. *The Contributor*, www.thecontributor.org.

17. John Parker, *The Contributor*, August 1–14, 2013, 3.

18. Wayne Sampe, *The Contributor*, April 25–May 8, 2013, 3.

19. Dale Carnegie, *The Little Recognized Secret of Success* (New York: Dale Carnegie and Associates, 1965).

20. Gayle, interview with author, May 30, 2013.

21. According to answers.com, this phrase means waiting for what comes next if it seems inevitable. Origin: old wooden buildings where every sound could be heard so if a shoe was being removed, often they got dropped and made a noisy clunk so you waited for the other one to drop before you relaxed again. (Answers.com, accessed September 18, 2014, www.answers.com/QWhat_does_the_phrase_'waiting_for_the_other_shoe_to_drop'_mean.)

22. Thomas Moore, "Come, Ye Disconsolate," 1816, Public Domain.

23. *Merriam-Webster's Collegiate Dictionary*, 11th ed., s.v. "joy," accessed September 18, 2014, www.merriam-webster.com/dictionary/joy.

24. Ibid.

25. "Arthur Robert Ashe, Jr.," Biography.com, 2014, www.biography.com/people/arthur-ashe-9190544.

26. "'Last Lecture' Professor Pausch Dies," CBS News, July 25, 2008, http://www.cbsnews.com/news/last-lecture-professor-pausch-dies.

27. Michael Hyatt, "5 Ways to Energize Your Team," MichaelHyatt.com, February 11, 2013. http://michaelhyatt.com/5-ways-to-energize-your-team.html.

28. Elisha A. Hoffman, "Is Your All on the Altar?" 1900, Public Domain.

29. *Merriam-Webster's Collegiate Dictionary*, 11th ed., s.v. "contented," accessed September 18, 2014, www.merriam-webster.com/dictionary/contented.

30. Hoffman, "Is Your All on the Altar?"

31. Urban Dictionary, www.urbandictionary.com, s.v. "Contentment," accessed September 18, 2014, www.urbandictionary.com/define.php?term=Contentment.

32. Sarah Ban Breathnach, *Simple Abundance: A Daybook of Comfort and Joy*, (New York: Warner Books, 1995), back cover.

33. Ibid, foreword.

34. Ibid.

35. Ibid.

36. Prince William, interviewed by Max Foster, CNN, August 19, 2013, www.cnn.com/2013/08/19/world/prince-william-transcript.

CHAPTER 2

Happiness Achieved?

By Cynthia A. Bond Hopson

The popular jingle for Coca-Cola, "I'd Like to Teach the World to Sing," paints a picture of happiness. Read the lyrics to the whole song, and you can easily conjure up a picture of snow-capped mountains, the big Montana sky, a wobbly-legged calf looking adoringly into her mother's eyes, giggling children romping in sprinklers in the heat of summer—and you do not just feel harmony and happiness, you taste it. Pure, simple, and deliciously wrapped with a bow dipped in chocolate.

Happiness is a magical journey that brings us into harmony with ourselves, our community, the world, nature, and with everything we treasure: spider webs in the morning dew, gorgeous sunsets we can almost touch, the beauty of a perfectly ripe Georgia peach, or the sweetness of a Hawaiian pineapple, still warm from the sun.

The pursuit of happiness brings us into harmony and solidarity with all of God's creation, with majestic creatures, both great and small, and allows us to seek, build, and live in the beloved community as the popular song-turned-jingle touts.

The story goes that McCann-Erickson advertising executive Bill Backer was traveling in Ireland with British songwriters Roger Cook and Billy Davis when their plane was delayed overnight. They noticed the next morning that all the hot tempers, rudeness, and frustration prompted by the previous night's inconvenience had been replaced with conversation, jokes and Coca-Cola. The rest is history.[1]

The song, dubbed by *Campaign* magazine as "one of the best-loved and most influential ads in TV history,"[2] got high marks because it married the idea of happiness and universal love for Coca-Cola into something people could feel and touch. The peace and solidarity espoused in the words invite every person to be happy, to hope, to be treated with kindness and dignity because of their inherent and sacred worth. It invites them to be part of something greater than themselves.

Happiness, as a state of mind, a dwelling place, a lofty pursuit, is a gift from God worth giving and receiving. We live it out in the environment through protecting our fragile ecosystems, conserving natural resources, and treating our precious resources as God treats us. For more than a generation now, school children have been taught to turn the water off while they brush their teeth and to recycle, renew, and reuse, especially everyday items that fill landfills globally.

In many locales, Boy Scout troops and students collect dated phone books from the community to recycle. Cool prizes like bicycles and video games inspire students to not just think about the eventual happiness that comes from winning but to participate in protecting the future they will inhabit.

Discussions rage on about the existence, legitimacy, or lack thereof of global warming, even as negotiations over dwindling water supplies and rights, the so-called new gold, threaten global stability, personal choices, and overall well-being. More than nine hundred participants from one hundred countries attended a recent United Nations International Water Conference in Dushanbe, Tajikistan, indicating the global significance of this issue. World Water Day provides facts about the increasing demands placed on our water resources that underscore the importance of this issue:

- 783 million people have no access to clean water and almost 2.5 billion do not have access to adequate sanitation;
- 6 to 8 million people die annually from the consequences of disasters and water-related diseases; and
- Global population growth projections of 2 to 3 billion people over the next forty years, combined with changing diets, result in a predicted increase in food demand of 70 percent by 2050.

These issues are interconnected—increasing agricultural output, for example, will substantially increase both water and energy consumption, leading to increased competition for water between water-using sectors.[3]

These important quality of life issues are inextricably linked with global warming, societal challenges, and governmental discussions surrounding happiness.

As a matter of fact, "The United Nations World Happiness Report 2013" puts forth the notion that happiness may be used as a measure of social progress and well-being, a driver of public policy and priority setting, and may also measure moral character. For policy makers, the key issue is what affects happiness. The report also shows the major beneficial side effects of happiness: happy people live longer, are more productive, earn more, and are also better citizens, so well-being should be developed both for its own sake and for its side effects.[4] The global report, sponsored by the UN's Sustainable Development Solutions Network, surveyed people in 156 countries and ranked their thoughts on wealth, health, freedom to make life choices, having someone to count on in times of trouble, freedom from corruption, and the generosity of fellow citizens.[5] The report's common themes also included these findings: (1) Money may not buy happiness but it helps; (2) more money means more problems; (3) being poor in certain places can be particularly rough; (4) nice weather doesn't correlate to happiness.[6]

Health, freedom to make life choices, and having someone to count on are three of the more personal findings of the report for most of us. This directly correlates with our daily and meaningful relationships—those people, places, and things we look forward to and make time for. Relationships enhance and enrich our lives and add intrinsic value. If you want to see a megawatt smile, talk to people about their friends and the time they spend together. Thankfully friendships and relationships cross almost every boundary and threshold to come in all sizes, ages, shapes, and from all kinds of places.

Country music's Garth Brooks bragged about his "Friends in Low Places" on a single from his best-selling *No Fences* album. The song that at first sounds like an apology and acceptance of blame for showing up in the wrong attire and being inappropriate, spent four weeks on the charts. The music video for "All My Rowdy Friends Are Coming Over Tonight," by legend "Rockin' Randall" Hank Williams, Jr., probably prompted many a keg of beer to be opened and more than a few pigs to be cooked in the ground in preparation for happy "friend" time.

Not only are friends a guaranteed, enormous, and immediate source of laughter, empathy, pride, and fun, they also help us live out the gospel. John 15:13 beautifully reminds us that "no one has greater love than this, to lay down one's life for one's friends." We can usually count on our friends to be honest about whether the dress is too tight or advise if the maybe-too-brown cookies should be eaten at home by the two of you or taken to the potluck. Bryn (not her real name) has cherished friends of all races and ethnicities and is teaching her children to love their friends without modifiers: "I believe if you have to define people by color, ethnicity, or size, they're not your friends. I love and treasure all the wonderful people who bless my life."[7]

Learning to be tolerant of difference, seeking new multi-ethnic experiences through immersion in other cultures, risking vulnerability, and developing partnerships outside your comfort zone help build community and deepen ties across cultures and ethnicities. Even when language poses a barrier, happiness and smiles come in all languages.

An organized life and order go hand-in-hand and, when done well, they bring enormous pleasure and happiness. You are never too old to set another goal, dream big dreams, or make good choices. Being happy is a worthwhile goal and one that's worthy of pursuit.

LIKE CINDERELLA, WE WILL LIVE HAPPILY EVER AFTER

Fairy tales do come true. There, we've said it and now we declare wicked stepmothers, stepsisters, witches, lonely towers, and frog princes off-limits. Nothing will deter us from our happily-ever-after destiny. We declare we will be happy in love and ready and willing to do the give-and-take a relationship requires to be successful.

If it were only that simple and easy—to declare and make it be so—many of today's first marriages would not end in divorce. Couples get married because they are in love or some reasonable representation of it. Hopefully they start with a fresh agenda, high hopes, and an illusion that they will live happily ever after in a castle of their own. When they get divorced, as happens more and more frequently these days, some of the reasons cited are loss of intimacy, poor communication, incompatibility, finances, outside influences, conflict, sexual incompatibility, and infidelity.

According to the Centers for Disease Control's National Vital Statistics System, in 2011, the rate per 1,000 in the total population in the United States for marriages and provisional number of marriages was 6.8 percent, while the rate for divorces and annulments was 3.6.[8] While it looks like half of all marriages end in divorce, this is much like saying watermelons are green and cucumbers are green, so all green things are fruits. Here's why this gets confusing. When statistics are collected for marriages and divorces, they are tallied annually, but the comparisons get skewed because the "half end in divorce" statements do not consider all the marriages that already exist and stay intact.

As people remain healthier and their life spans increase, couples are reaching remarkable milestone anniversaries. An article in the *Huffington Post* announced the end of the eighty-three-year marriage of a Detroit couple. When Victoria Wrubel died, she had been married to her husband Steven since 1929 and the couple had no children.[9] Victoria and Steven married at age 18 and 20, respectively, much younger than the median age at first marriage nowadays, which is 25.8 for women and 28.3 for men between the ages of 15 and 44.[10]

There were no secrets shared about how the Wrubel's marriage survived so many years, but chances are they negotiated who would do what, when, and how much like Mel and Joey Schwanke of Fremont, Nebraska. The couple, married sixty-five years, owned a flower shop for more than sixty years and started wearing coordinated outfits about halfway through. They have one hundred forty-six custom-made matching outfits they have been rotating over the course of thirty-five years. The customary way they handle it is Mel wears a tie to match Joey's dress—she picks out the matching combinations and they don't "dare go somewhere without having matching outfits."[11]

From handsome princes, glass slippers, and mice-drawn carriages for Cindy E. Rella-Jones to thousands of cups of coffee and Sunday newspapers for Steven and Victoria Wrubel to matching outfits for Joey and Mel Schwanke at lunch, church, and work, happily ever after rocks!

ENDNOTES

1. "The 'Hilltop' Ad: The Story of a Commercial," Coca-Cola Advertisting Television Home Page, accessed September 14, 2014, http://memory.loc.gov/ammem/ccmphtml/colaadv.html.

2. James Hamilton and John Tylee, "Ten ads that changed advertising," *Campaign*, May 18, 2007, www.campaignlive.co.uk/news/658586.

3. "World Water Day 2013: International Year of Water Cooperation," UNESCO, www.unwater.org/water-cooperation-2013/water-cooperation/facts-and-figures/en.

4. UNSDSN.org, "World Happiness Report 2013," eds. John Helliwell, Richard Layard, and Jeffrey Sachs, http://unsdsn.org/wp-content/uploads/2014/02/WorldHappinessReport2013_online.pdf.

5. Roff Smith. "Five Takeaways from the UN's Global Report on Happiness." *National Geographic*, September 9, 2013.

6. Ibid.

7. Bryn, Interview with author, July 10, 2013.

8. "National Marriage and Divorce Rate Trends," Center for Disease Control and Prevention, National Vital Statistics System, February 19, 2013, www.cdc.gov/nchs/nvss/marriage_divorce_tables.htm.

9. "Longest-Married Couple: 83-Year Marriage Ends After Wife's Death," *The Huffington Post*, updated April 12, 2013, http://www.huffingtonpost.com/2013/04/11/longest-married-couple_n_3062396.html.

10. Casey E. Copen, Kimberly Daniels, et al., "First Marriages in the United States: Data From the 2006–2010 National Survey of Family Growth," National Health Statistics Reports, No. 49, March 22, 2012, www.cdc.gov/nchs/data/nhsr/nhsr049.pdf.

11. Eric Pfeiffer, "Nebraska couple wear matching outfits every day for 35 years," *Yahoo! News*, May 29, 2012, http://news.yahoo.com/blogs/sideshow/nebraska-cou.

CHAPTER 3

Culture and Happiness

By Cynthia A. Bond Hopson

Think for just a moment about that box of Wheaties, "the Breakfast of Champions," you bought because the fortified flakes would make you capable of winning Wimbledon like tennis great Althea Gibson. Perhaps it was the Clairol Loving Care Hair jingle that said blondes have more fun than darned near anybody else. And, because everyone wants to have fun, we should all strive to become blonde. It's Lady Clairol if we're thrifty, that is.

If we're not thrifty shoppers and want to feel really special, we should splurge on the L'Oréal brand. Yes, it costs more, but we're worth it. If you buy this product or that one, you'll have clearer skin, longer lashes, less pungent perspiration, more dates, more beautiful feet, better smelling breath, and an "ultimate driving machine." If you plan well, you will have enough leftover insurance money to buy a pig that drives a convertible, a flight to wherever pigs fly, and the list goes on. There is no way that money can't buy happiness—media and advertising pretty much say so.

Advertising is perhaps the single most influential force in helping us shape our perceptions and thoughts about cultural norms, who we are, what makes us important, and what we aspire to have and be. Anyone who thinks or believes they are not affected by this constant barrage of mind-altering, culture-shifting messaging probably has not given the topic much thought.

In *Mythmakers: Gospel, Culture and the Media*, author William F. Fore confirms that the media do affect us profoundly, and we can better understand how the media affect our values and worldview if we look at the changes throughout history.[1] The evolution of technology and twenty-four-hour news cycles have the potential to exacerbate and overexpose unsuspecting and vulnerable audiences to negative and/or problematic influences.

Multiple studies have shown that if children watch repeated violence, they may become desensitized to its negative effects and come to see aggressive and deadly behavior as normal. Further, according to *Killing Us Softly*, Jean Kilbourne's groundbreaking work that covers nearly four decades on the media and gender representation in advertising, the long-term effects of advertising on the images and psyche of women can be dangerous and life-altering in terms of objectification, feelings of powerlessness, and the selling of externally produced "happiness."

Her third iteration of *Killing Us Softly*, a collection of multimedia ads that point to the problems and unrealistic expectations set forth through media, poignantly and painfully explore the objectification of women and how it can negatively affect body image, self-concept, and esteem. She concludes that advertising may trivialize sex, offer pornography as mainstream, minimize the importance of relationships, and lead to health-related illnesses like anorexia.[2]

Media theorists continue to debate whether media reflect, shape, or mirror societal norms, and research consistently shows different kinds of content have different effects that are often colored by audience needs and organizational pressures. Pamela J. Shoemaker and Stephen D. Reese contend that the mass media shape, pound, constrain, and encourage the content by a multitude of forces.[3] If this is so, then it is probable that the coverage may not reflect reality at all.

Nowadays, with the proliferation of reality shows, we see up close and personal all the happiness money can buy coupled with personal and group dysfunction disguised as normalcy, friendly competition, and entertainment. One week it's Khloe Kardashian and Lamar Odom, who tried to hold together their crumbling marriage amid rumors of drug addiction and infidelity. A few years back it was golfer Tiger Woods who fell from his squeaky-clean pedestal and shattered his "perfect superstar, Mr. Good Guy" image; he still shows the lingering effects of the embarrassment, public disgrace, and humiliation.

Real homemakers of virtually every city are cringing at the spectacle being made of the rich and famous "housewives" who want us to see how great they have it in their beautiful, elaborately decorated homes. Most seem catty, petty, and immature, but their ratings indicate that many want to know how the "other half" lives.

Fueled by the Internet and an obvious pop culture thirst for the intimate details of rural Southern families, overnight fame and fortune has come to the Shannon/Thompson family of McIntyre, Georgia. Honey Boo Boo, the cherubic star for whom the show is named, her parents, Mama June and Sugar Bear, and the crew on *Here Comes Honey Boo Boo*, could be an updated version of the popular Clampett family of cornbread- and possum-eating fame from the 1960s TV series *The Beverly Hillbillies*.

The Clampetts' antics offered and indelibly cemented a plethora of stereo-types about money-grabbing bankers, simple-minded mountaineers, and Southerners that some areas and actors have never outlived. They were genuinely in culture shock in the big city, and their gullibility and complete innocence provided laughs for peak audiences during most of their nine seasons on network television.

Alana Thompson, Honey Boo Boo's given name, is proud of her "redneck" heritage, and she and her family film the show in and around their modest Georgia home, complete with captions translating their unique dialect. While Granny, *The Beverly Hillbillies'* feisty matriarch, stopped to retrieve dead animals for her stews, this family's antics include making public comments about bodily functions, reveling in unusual dietary habits (a favorite is "sketti," Mama June's spaghetti concoction made with three sticks of butter and ketchup), and the family washing their hair in the kitchen sink.

The Internet offers footage of students around the country watching and critiquing episodes of *Here Comes Honey Boo Boo* as part of their study of pop culture. Alana, whose "a dolla makes me holla" mantra made her a *Toddlers and Tiaras* pageant favorite, provided raucous entertainment as she prepared for her debut in a major pageant. She and her family attended a local festival where the recreation included bobbing for raw pig's feet and mud-wallowing contests.

Viewers of the Honey Boo Boo show commented on how happy this family is and how much they seem to enjoy being together. They literally bask in each other's presence. Talk show host Wendy Williams interviewed Mama June in July 2013 and also commented on how much love and care she sees in the family when she watches this show.[4]

Much of pop culture and many of the media images driving the quest for happiness-inspired riches and fame are prompted by celebrities and their glamorous or notorious lifestyles, coupled with advertisements for high-status products that transform regular people into cool stars and superheroes.

Country singer Brad Paisley scored a megahit with "Online," a song about how an average guy gets transformed into a highly sought after hunk when he signs into his computer account. In real life, he's asthmatic, drives an old car, is short, overweight, works at a local pizza parlor, and has only been to California as part of the high school marching band's appearance at the Rose Parade. Online and in the computer dating world, which often encourages anonymity and mystery, he's single and rich, a Karate expert, drives a Maserati, is a Calvin Klein model, and poses for *Gentlemen's Quarterly*. The music video of the song won Paisley the award for Best Video at the 2007 Country Music Association Awards.

Much of this entertainment and many of these videos and shows are labeled "reality," though it remains unclear whose reality is being promoted and celebrated with the extravagance, perfect bodies, pettiness, catfights, and focus on bad behavior. Companies are shelling out billions on ads for new cars, homes, dating and marriage sites, insurance to prevent mayhem, soft drinks, and prescription medication designed to fix almost any problem. So far there are no magic potions or bottles of happiness available for purchase, though they would be hot commodities and in great demand if an increasingly divided and segmented viewership is ever exposed en masse to the possibility.

Guarding impressionable children from troubling images has never been more important or difficult as attention spans shrink and busy parents resort to television and electronics as a steady stream of entertainment for pacifying increasingly sophisticated children. Further, the Parents Television Council reports these statistics that skew the equation regarding affluence, aspirations, the power of media images of happiness and normalcy, and their long-term effects:

- By age 18, a U.S. youth will have seen 16,000 simulated murders and 200,000 acts of violence.
- Approximately 40 percent of families with preschoolers own video game equipment.
- Two-thirds of children in the United States have televisions in their bedrooms.
- More than 58 percent of children surveyed (ages 14 to 17) report having seen a pornographic site on the Internet or on their phone.
- 37 percent have received a link to sexually explicit content.
- More than 98 percent of homes had at least one television in 2007.
- Children spend more time watching television than in any other activity except sleep.
- Television reaches children at a younger age and for more time than any other socializing institution except the family.[5]

Decency, civility, and culture may come to a crossroads as increased media influence, power, and money fuel the pursuit of love and happiness. While money can't buy love and happiness, it can be spent on almost everything else.

"MONEY IS A GREAT SERVANT BUT DON'T LET IT BE YOUR MASTER."
—Ana Weber, author of *The Money Flow*[6]

Doctors, lawyers, police officers, hospitals . . . Nashville, Las Vegas, Dallas, Boston, New York, Chicago . . . power, influence, corruption, and more power . . . Turn on your television or go to the movies and you will likely see people in these professions, in these cities, struggling with these topics. The media show us how the "other half" lives and this newly created need for new things drives ambition and capitalism in its purest form—they create a need and then fill it. When we're inspired to buy, somebody has to sell something; companies make money from our inspiration to spend more. They create a need, and we succumb.

Ana Weber offers the poignant reminder above about not becoming a servant to our money and the things we crave and ultimately acquire or continue to long for. She suggests that changing our attitudes about money, how we acquire, spend, and respect it, is critical as we seek and pursue happiness.

Are you someone who grew up during the Great Depression and still worry about running out of money? Have immigration, health, or age restrictions tested and affected your ability to be self-sufficient and independent as you go about doing the things you enjoy? Have you set commonsense financial goals for where you want to be next and strategies for how you plan to get there?

Savings and financial advocates advise women in particular to pay closer attention to their money and how it affects their physical health and long-range personal choices. Wealth Coach Deborah Owens encourages women to become more investment savvy and to take control of their lives and purses by leveraging their intuition, creativity, and empathy as they build personal wealth.[7]

If you're planning to finance happiness, the question becomes how much does it cost, anyway? In terms of dollars and cents, there is of course no way to know definitively since definition, starting points, and desired outcomes vary from person to person. As you would imagine, a simple reply might be MasterCard's signature answer: "Priceless." In addition to these factors, determination and persistence are also priceless, but surprisingly, in a 2010 Princeton report, researchers found that money could indeed buy some happiness but only after reaching $75,000 in annual income. After that amount, money wasn't a factor in being happy or not, but earning more helped people feel better about their lives and bolstered their sense of being successful. The researchers discovered that with improved incomes people viewed their lives more positively, but the quality of their everyday experiences—their feelings—did not improve after that income threshold.[8]

If their income dropped to less than $75,000, less money was associated with emotional pain and the lack of ability to do what mattered most in terms of their emotional well-being—things like spending time with friends and family, avoiding pain and disease, and leisure activities.[9] There is no indication that these researchers looked at those living below the poverty level or those who make significantly less than $75,000. An August 2013 Marist College poll said $50,000 (60 million U.S. households earn this much or more) may be the tipping point when it comes to personal happiness and satisfaction with life. Those with incomes over $50,000 cite a better quality of life in every category measured, including housing, health, finances, and free time.[10]

The poll, which looked at the quality of life across generations, found that for Americans with household incomes less than $50,000 (93 million households) their financial situation spills over to shape a generally negative view of their future and life—they're more likely to say they're not happy and more worried about becoming a burden to their families.[11]

A September 2013 *USA Today* article asks, "What is the formula for happiness?" Again, no magic bullets appear, but the formula includes things like listening to your mother about rest, decision-making and choices, embracing diversity, and understanding that some stress and quick adaptability to change are good in new situations.[12] No studies reported on the cost of peace of mind, a usual aftereffect of being happy and contented, though Ryan Howell, a San Francisco State assistant psychology professor, supports findings from data found in the Happiness Project that simply espouse "If you want to be happy, spend $5 on a friend, not $20 on yourself."[13]

Whatever happiness he could have derived from following the research's altruistic suggestions and findings were hopelessly lost when he succumbed to his temptations and had donuts and Danishes instead of taking a friend to lunch.[14]

Other advice on finding happiness includes pet ownership or even being near dogs—no matter what kind of day you've had, your dog is always happy to see you. The mere act of petting a dog can cause a positive chain reaction according to *USA Today*'s Steve Dale: "Instantly, neurotransmitters in our heads do a happy dance—it's involuntary. We feel good."[15] Dale says feeling good leads to smiling, which leads to lower blood pressure and decreased stress and anxiety. These neurotransmitters also help us heal faster, thus multiplying the benefits gained.[16]

While pet ownership can be expensive, the benefits seem to far outweigh the outlay, especially when compared to the costs of impulse shopping done to assuage loneliness, depression, disappointment, and other emotional shortcomings. Experts agree that impulse buying is a hard habit to break, but it is one of the things people do to make themselves "happy." A 2013 *USA Weekend* article shared dated but disturbing statistics on impulse shopping: in the late '90s, North Americans spent more than $4 billion a year on impulse purchases.[17] In 2012, Americans spent $10.7 trillion on beer, pretzels, over-the-counter teeth whiteners, sinus treatments, and celebrating St. Patrick's Day.[18] Globally, consumer spending is not nearly so frivolous because of limited resources, disease, rampant poverty, and famine.

A 2012 article in the *BBC News Magazine* reported that the total value of world income is about $70 trillion annually for the world's seven billion people. The average income might be about $10,000 per person per year, but everyone doesn't have a job, some are children, and the cost of living and population varies from country to country, skewing the purchasing power of wage earners. In real terms however, more than a third of the world's population lives on less than two dollars a day.[19]

Analysts also believe that with the increase in global consumer prices and the prevalence of home-shopping networks and online shopping, spending has shifted significantly. The economic downturn and slow but steady recovery has affected spending on every level, especially impacting the ratio of discretionary spending versus what is spent on necessities.

Though the causes for impulse shopping are varied and often complicated, at the heart of much of it is the lure of a quick fix that makes people happy and boosts their self-esteem. For others, it is the thrill of the sale or deal and the "huge" savings that result. Impulse buying staves off depression and anger. Like petting your dog releases an emotional change, so does impulse buying. If left unchecked, impulse buying can become compulsive buying, which psychologists agree is more chronic, more difficult to resist, and more financially destructive. Shopping with the children also leads to impulsive and compulsive buying. Internet shopping can prove extremely destructive and dangerous for senior citizens who face mobility challenges, loneliness, and limited or fixed incomes.

The media continue to be a major economic and emotional driver for powerful images of upwardly mobile aspirations, status, happiness, personal and professional satisfaction, and overall well-being.

United Methodist Women members have been engaged in monitoring media images of women since the 1970s, calling for a fair and accurate representation of female images promoting just, participatory, equitable, and sustainable media and communication technologies, and participating in alternative media and communication efforts to foster balanced gender representation.

Serene Jones, a pastor and president of Union Theological Seminary, New York, says, "More than any other social barometer, our advertisements illuminate the defining spirit of our moment." Jones asks her readers to examine what influences them: ". . . look at our culture, yearnings, and discern why meaningless things like soft drinks and cars have taken over our language of social justice and love." She asks, "What are we to do in a world where corporations have assumed the voice of social justice?"[20]

The commercialization of spiritual values and the attachment of those values to products for sale needs to be resisted through constant critical thinking, monitoring, engagement in social action, and the creation of alternative media. One such alternative media is United Methodist Women's **response** magazine.

Engaging in advocacy work is a key. *The Book of Resolutions of The United Methodist Church 2012* contains a couple of key resolutions on the use of media. "Proper Use of Communication Technologies" urges leaders to "preach and teach about the impact of media on the quality of life and values of individuals and society and to suggest ways congregations and individuals can both work with the positive forces and resist the negative," and also encourages the members of faith communities to "advocate for technologies that allow consumers to exclude unwanted commercial messages . . ."[21]

Happiness then is counteracting false notions of happiness that are tied to products that promote consumer desires and form acquisition instincts, addressing them at personal and corporate levels, and making a conscious choice to participate in the happiness intended for us by our Creator.

The pursuit of happiness is the chase of a lifetime

"Pursuit: an activity that one engages in as a vocation, profession, or avocation,"[22] says Merriam-Webster online. (By permission. From *Merriam-Webster's Collegiate® Dictionary, 11th edition*, ©2014 by Merriam-Webster, Inc., www.merriam-webster.com.) In dramas on television and in the movies, police cruisers careen down city streets and interstates in hot pursuit of crooks and bad guys in cooler, faster cars.

"You'll never take me alive, copper,"[23] the infamous line from James Cagney's role in the movie *The Public Enemy* (1931), reminds us that not all pursuits end in the capture or acquisition of whatever was being chased. Sometimes intangibles like power, riches, status, and other hard to attain and maintain entities elude us in a very real way although we are surrounded by all the outward trappings and obvious accoutrements to be successful in our chase.

Globally, we see leaders who exploit and oppress their people and live extravagantly on the profits from diamonds, oil, and other natural resources while the poor barely eke out a living, yet many are able to find joy in life.

"LIFE, LIBERTY, AND THE PURSUIT OF HAPPINESS"— DOES IT MEAN CHASING, STRIVING, AND SURVIVING?

"We hold these truths to be self-evident, that all men are created equal, that they are endowed by their Creator with certain unalienable Rights, that among these are Life, Liberty and the pursuit of Happiness."[24] These familiar lines, from the founding fathers of the United States in the Declaration of Independence, continue to inspire generations and be a borderless and boundless beacon of hope for the masses.

Whether it looks like the American dream—the ability to pull yourself up by your bootstraps, own a home, find meaningful work you love, and the freedom to move effortlessly and safely toward prosperity and entrepreneurship—or the eternal optimist's dream of self-determination and the means to provide hope and opportunity for yourselves and your loved ones, the pursuit of happiness is a cherished right and a venture worthy of the efforts expended.

While lofty and far-reaching, this seemingly insightful and inclusive line was originally exclusive to "all (white) men" and additional provisions had to be put into place to include rights and access for women and people of color to level the playing field. Life and liberty are self-explanatory—we can see, touch and feel them. In some instances, the two can be so powerful, we can actually become heroes and martyrs because of them.

In the case of the late former South African president Nelson Mandela, life and liberty became his cause célèbre, and an international movement that ended apartheid was born. Imprisoned as a young freedom fighter against a legacy of racism, poverty, and strife, he endured confinement for more than twenty-seven years in his quest for liberty and justice. People around the world joined in his struggle for freedom and celebrated when he was released and ultimately preached peace and reconciliation, not hate and retaliation, as he became the nation's first black South African to hold office.

Life and liberty rarely need amplification or embellishment—everyone deserves to live freely and as they choose, but this "pursuit of happiness" concept begs individual interpretation, inspiration, and implementation for it to become a living, breathing entity worthy of energy and investment. While what motivates a mother of four to complete hours of Habitat for Humanity classes and sweat equity to become a first-time home owner is probably not that different from the wrongly accused prisoner who studies law and writes letters daily declaring his innocence, at the heart of their inspiration is the possibility of happiness, a fulfilling life, and personal freedom.

The question then becomes: is pursuing happiness a byproduct of their initial quest for a better life? Perhaps. Is it a gateway to the chase that ends in satisfaction and fulfillment, and persistence that produces the silver lining they are taught to strive for? Probably. Or is it sheer will, persistence, and the possibility of success that keeps them going in their pursuit? Most likely it is all of the above. Is happiness what God wants for us and do we get to it through perseverance?

Dale Earnhardt was one of the most widely known and well-compensated NASCAR drivers on the circuit, but much of his success came after a rocky start. Earnhardt eventually won six national championships for Richard Childress Racing because even when he didn't finish first he refused to be defeated. When he lost, he worked harder. Childress said, "You can't always wait for the storm to pass, sometimes you have to work in the rain."[25]

Rain, sleet, hail, high water, sacrifice, defeat, and calamity are all part of the pursuit-of-happiness puzzle and equation. Faith, coupled with bravery, courage, and fortitude born from submission and surrender to God's will for your life, means the chase of a lifetime becomes the ultimate victory. Chapter 4 will help us to grapple more extensively with the biblical and gospel lessons surrounding happiness and our faithfulness to God.

ENDNOTES

1. William F. Fore, *Mythmakers: Gospel, Culture and the Media* (New York: Friendship Press, 1990), Chapter 3.

2. Jean Kilbourne, *Killing Us Softly 3, Advertising's Image of Women* (Northhampton, MA: Media Education Foundation, 2000), DVD.

3. Pamela J. Shoemaker and Stephen D. Reese, *Mediating the Message: Theories of Influences on Mass Media Content* (New York: Longman, 1991), 24.

4. *The Wendy Williams Show*, "Mama June," *The Wendy Williams Show* video, 11:08, July 17, 2013, www.wendyshow.com/2013/07/17/mama-june-honey-boo-boo.

5. "Facts and TV Statistics," Parents Television Council, w2.parentstv.org/main/research/facts.aspx.

6. Ana Weber, as quoted by Cheryl Alkon in "Money: Go with the Flow," *USA Weekend*, July 12–14, 2013, 4.

7. Deborah Owens and Brenda Lane Richardson, *A Purse of Your Own: An Easy Guide to Financial Security* (New York: Touchstone, 2009).

8. Daniel Kahneman and Angus Deaton, "High income improves evaluation of life but not emotional well-being," Proceedings of the National Academy of Sciences of the United States of America, August 4, 2010, www.pnas.org/content/107/38/16489.

9. Ibid.

10. "Generation to Generation: Money Matters," Marist College Institute for Public Opinion, August 13, 2013, http://maristpoll.marist.edu/wp-content/misc/Home%20instead/Money%20Matters_April%202012_FINAL.pdf.

11. Ibid.

12. Anita Bruzzese, "On the Job: What Is the Formula for Happiness?" *USA Today*, September 1, 2013, www.usatoday.com/story/money/columnist/bruzzese/2013/09/01/on-the-job-workplace-happiness/2736211.

13. Ryan T. Howell, "How Much Does Happiness Cost? Not Much." *Psychology Today*, April 21, 2012, www.psychologytoday.com/blog/cant-buy-happiness/201204/how-much-does-happiness-cost-not-much.

14. Ibid.

15. Steve Dale, "How Dogs Spread Happiness," *USA Today*, January 24, 2012, http://usatoday30.usatoday.com/news/health/wellness/pets/story/2012-01-24/How-dogs-spread-happiness/52756792/1.

16. Ibid.

17. Jeff Wuorio, "I'll Take That, and That, and That." *USA Weekend*, July 12–14, 2013, www.usaweekend.com/apps/pbcs.dll/article?AID=2013307120006.

18. Lucas Reilly, "By the Numbers: How Americans Spend Their Money," July 17, 2012, http://mentalfloss.com/article/31222/numbers-how-americans-spend-their-money.

19. Ruth Alexander, "Where Are You on the Global Pay Scale?" *BBC News Magazine*, March 29, 2012, www.bbc.com/news/magazine-17512040.

20. Serene Jones, "Selling Social Justice Short," *Time*, February 14, 2014, http://time.com/7359/selling-social-justice-short.

21. "Proper Use of Communication Technologies," Resolution #8016, *The Book of Resolutions of The United Methodist Church* (Nashville: United Methodist Publishing House, 2012), 162. III. C.

22. *Merriam-Webster's Collegiate Dictionary*, 11th ed., s.v. "pursuit," accessed September 18, 2014, www.merriamwebster.com/dictionary/pursuit.

23. Kubic Glasmon, John Bright, and Harvey F. Thew. *The Public Enemy*, directed by William A. Wellman, Warner Bros. Pictures, 1931.

24. "The Declaration of Independence," US History.org, www.ushistory.org/declaration/document.

25. Julia Savacool, "Find the silver lining in hard times," *USA Weekend*, November 9–11, 2012, 5.

CHAPTER 4

Biblical Happiness

By Sarah Heaner Lancaster

God cares about our happiness. We know this to be true because the Bible talks about happiness. In saying this, though, it is important to realize that the happiness God cares about is not always the same happiness that we think that we want. It is not the happiness that is shaped by advertising or the media, or even simply what is studied by researchers. This part of our study will be looking at the Bible and the theology of our United Methodist tradition to better understand the kind of happiness that God desires for us, and how we can become happy in a way that pleases God.

The kind of happiness that can be called biblical has two sides to it. First, as we would expect, it names a feeling of contentment and satisfaction. Second, it is contentment or satisfaction that God evaluates as good. In other words, just because we feel content does not mean we are happy in the way God cares about. The Bible also shows us what kind of contentment God wants for us. Biblical happiness, then, is a feeling, but it is not just any good feeling. It is a feeling that comes from doing what pleases God.

The two sides of biblical happiness can be seen more clearly when reading different translations of the Bible in English. The Old Testament was written originally in Hebrew and the New Testament was written originally in Greek. Sometimes one word can have several very different meanings—think of how the word "light" in English can mean both "not heavy" and "not dark." A different language may not have a single word that means all the same things, so some associations may be lost when the word is translated. Translators have to make a choice about what to say, but that choice may hide other options. Reading different translations where translators made different choices can help us see what was lost.

For instance, the first word of Psalm 119 is translated in the New Revised Standard Version (NRSV) as "happy." The New International Version (NIV), though, translates it as "blessed." Together, these words show the two sides of biblical happiness. For God to bless a person shows that God favors that person and evaluates what they are doing as good. This is the idea that is stressed in the NIV. The word in Hebrew, though, also means this person is happy, and this is the idea stressed in the NRSV. One word in English does not say both things to us, so translators pick one or the other. To understand what "happy" and "blessed" meant, though, to the writers of the Bible, we have to think of both at the same time. We will see as we examine the Bible and our tradition just how closely related those ideas are.

HAPPINESS IN THE LAW

Already in the Old Testament, the Bible makes clear that God's favor and human fulfillment come from living according to God's commandments. The two great commandments that Jesus endorses in Matthew 22:37–39 are the essence of the law given to Israel on Mt. Sinai. Deuteronomy 6:5 says, "You shall love the Lord your God with all your heart, and with all your soul, and with all your might," and this is the essence of the first commandment that Jesus names. The second commandment that Jesus names is found in Leviticus 19:18. Far from being isolated commandments that Jesus simply liked the best, they serve as good orientation points to the structure of the Ten Commandments. The first four of the Ten Commandments prescribe the way to honor God properly. The next six commandments govern human relationships (honor your parents, do not steal, do not bear false witness, do not kill, etc.). These are ways of showing love to your neighbors. As Jesus indicates, all the law and the prophets hang on these ideas. In other words, what we read in the Old Testament, no matter how detailed and tedious it may seem, is intended to help us know how to love God and to love our neighbors.

Jesus' answer to the lawyer not only shows how he understood the Hebrew Scriptures, it has also often been taken as a summary of his own message and life. So Christian theologians have understood that the Old Testament and New Testament alike tell us to love God and to love your neighbor. Deuteronomy 30 explains that following God's commandments is a choice for life. Following them will lead to life and prosperity, ignoring them will lead to death and adversity (30:15–20). The covenant that God made with Israel was intended to be a blessing to Israel, because living in the way God calls us to live allows us to thrive. Israel understood that following God's commandments is righteousness, putting us in right relationship with God.

Although the entire law aims at the fulfillment that comes through obedience, theologian Ellen Charry argues that there is a category of commands in the Old Testament that are specifically meant to promote human flourishing because they cultivate wisdom in us. She calls these commands *asherist* (*asher* is the Hebrew word for happy and blessed).[1] *Asherist* commands include commands that govern all human relationships, for instance, the commands not to steal or swear falsely, and laws that specifically govern how to treat the poor and resident aliens (Leviticus 19:9–13). They also include laws about how to use the land and its fruits (Leviticus 25:3–5; 18–22). When we obey God's commands for the flourishing of the community, we not only revere God but also learn the values that God holds for the community.

By making those values our own, we become wise and discerning. With this wisdom, we are able to approach new situations in ways that honor God. In other words, when we face new circumstances not anticipated by a particular command, we are able to respond to them in a way God would approve because we have learned what God values. For instance, a law about leaving some grapes in a vineyard for the poor mentions specific behavior for an agrarian society. Even though our society is now more industrial and techno-logical, we may learn from this law the value of making sure the poor have access to the resources they need to live. This lesson is just as important for a society with few vineyards as it is for one with many.

These *asherist* commands especially show that the point of the law is not le-galism. The law aims to help us gain wisdom that can be exercised in creative and discerning judgment. Obedience to the law is not just about following rules; rather it leads to socialization and education in the ways of God so the community may thrive. Charry defines happiness as "enjoying God, creation, and self by cultivating the wisdom behind divine commands that enable one to become an instrument of the world's flourishing." In short, it is "godly self-enjoyment."[2]

HAPPINESS IN THE PSALMS

Some of the Psalms talk about how obedience to God's law leads to this hap-piness. In fact, the introduction to the entire Psalter sets up this idea. Psalm 1 opens the Psalter with the Hebrew word *asher*. This word may be translated as "happy," but because it also indicates favor, it can also be translated as "blessed." God favors, or God is pleased with, those who do not take the path of sin but instead study the law, meditate on it, allow themselves to be formed by it, and internalize its values. They become strong and fruitful trees.

Notice, too, this study is a "delight." So the happiness gained in study of the law brings not only external validation by God but also internal personal enjoyment. This psalm shows the two sides of biblical happiness. An excel-lent life, one that is judged by God to be good, also brings personal reward and satisfaction.

Psalm 1 talks about the law the way that Deuteronomy does: those who study and follow the law will prosper and those who do not will perish. The choice between life and death that Deuteronomy presents is also expressed here.

These ideas are also echoed in Psalm 112 and Psalm 119. The testimony of these psalms is that a life that keeps God's commands is a life well lived and satisfying. God blesses those who follow in God's ways.

But the psalms are also realistic. They recognize that sometimes the wicked seem to prosper at least for a time. Even though Psalm 1 speaks of the happiness of those who follow the law, the very next psalm acknowledges the threat to Israel from other nations. Psalm 2 ends with affirming trust in God: "Happy are all who take refuge in him." Even in adversity, trust in God leads to happiness. Several more psalms of struggle follow. It seems clear that loving and following the law does not mean adversity will be avoided, but rather that the relationship we have with God, cultivated by contemplation of God's law, helps us to endure the adversity that comes.

Even without using the word "happy," Psalm 19 focuses on happiness in God. Creation itself glorifies and enjoys God. God's care for and involvement in creation is evident in verses 1–6, but God's care for and involvement with Israel is the topic of the rest of the psalm. The law that God gives is perfect, and its benefits to those who follow it are clear: reviving the soul, making wise the simple, rejoicing the heart, enlightening the eyes. The law is desirable and sweet, and keeping it is rewarding. This psalm ends not only with an affirmation of God's faithfulness, but with a prayer that we may be faithful.

The psalms also acknowledge, though, that humans will not always be faithful, so they include confession of sin, both for the people as a whole (Psalm 106) and for individuals (Psalm 51). God is more faithful to the people than the people are to God, and God's steadfastness is reason for praise and rejoicing. Because of God's faithfulness to the covenant, it is possible to repent and return to God. God forgives and restores to right relationship. Knowing we are forgiven makes us happy and glad of heart (Psalm 32:1–2).

The psalms are full of language about many emotions, and if you read through them guided by Psalm 1, you can see both the happiness in God that comes from living an upright life and the struggle to be upright in the face of adversity, or even when other people mock your efforts to remain upright. You can also see the pain of falling away from relationship with God, and the happiness of returning to God. The psalms not only acknowledge happiness but also the obstacles to it. They also encourage hope. They show that being happy in God is not simplistic, but they also show how happiness in God is possible even when life is complex and messy.

HAPPINESS IN THE GOSPELS

We have already seen how Jesus understood the law, and he also spoke specifically about happiness in the way the law does. This can be seen by looking at some of his sayings recorded in Matthew 5:1–11 and Luke 6:20–22. Like the Hebrew word *asher,* the Greek word *makarios* means both "happy" and "blessed." Although Matthew and Luke record slightly different versions of what Jesus said, they both use the word *makarios* to begin his sayings. These verses are called the beatitudes because when the Bible was translated into Latin, the word used to translate *makarios* was *beatus,* which also means both "happy" and "blessed." Many English translations of the beatitudes use "blessed" to begin each saying, but some translations (for instance, the Good News Translation) begin with the word "happy." When John Wesley translated and wrote notes to the New Testament for his Methodist preachers, he began each beatitude with "happy." The reason for his choice of "happy" in this translation will become clear in the next chapter as we explore his understanding of happiness.

Most likely, the word "blessed" is preferred by many translators because it seems confusing to describe those who mourn or who are persecuted as happy. However, if we keep in mind the way the psalms talk about the complex messiness of life, we can more easily see why Jesus' words in the beatitudes reflect both sides of biblical happiness. These sayings not only tell us whom God favors, but also that these favored persons will be fulfilled.

For instance, the ones who mourn are not lighthearted while they are mourning, but in Matthew's version God blesses them by comforting them. The comfort that God provides is the surest comfort possible, so it brings deep and lasting fulfillment. The vision that Revelation 21:4 gives us of how God prevails over evil is that God "will wipe every tear from their eyes," and "mourning and crying and pain will be no more." That comfort is a genuine and lasting blessing, fulfilling our deepest longing to suffer no more. Luke's version suggests that lightheartedness may not be forever lost to those who weep because God will bless them with laughter.

Similarly, persecution for the sake of righteousness is not a pleasant experience, but the blessing God gives to those who are persecuted is the kingdom of heaven. The persecuted may rejoice and be glad knowing that they will be fulfilled with what the righteous want most, namely to do God's will even in difficult situations. We have records in Christian history of people who faced persecution unto death with this kind of gladness. One such story tells of two women who were martyred. Their names were Perpetua and Felicitas, which together mean "perpetual happiness."[3]

Keeping in mind that these sayings of Jesus call to mind happiness as much as blessing pushes us to go beyond superficial understandings of happiness to something deeper. Biblical happiness is not simply feeling pleasure, being in a good mood, or having fun. Biblical happiness is about being deeply fulfilled as a human being because we have trusted in our relationship with God to provide what we need the most. Adversity may be able to destroy a good mood, but for the faithful, it does not destroy confidence in God.

When he translated the New Testament, John Wesley used the word "happy" to begin each beatitude because he understood these sayings to be Jesus' instructions for "the complete art of happiness." Wesley says that rather than giving us commands, Jesus gently suggests to us what our duty is by telling us what will make us happy. He could read these sayings as instructions and not just statements about who was blessed because he interpreted them in light of his understanding of the way of salvation. For instance, Wesley took "poor in spirit" to refer to a penitent spirit and he understood those who mourn to be mourning for their sins.[4]

Even if his interpretations may not have been exactly what Jesus meant, Wesley surely sees something of importance when he recognizes that the beatitudes suggest a way of life. Certainly in Matthew's version, we can see how hungering and thirsting for righteousness, being merciful and pure in heart, and acting as peacemakers are qualities that should be cultivated as Christians. Other beatitudes do not seem to suggest Christian qualities as much as situations to be endured. Luke's version especially tends in that direction because he talks about concrete hunger and poverty instead of something spiritual. Still, even in those situations, we can see from the beatitudes that negative circumstances may be endured because we may hope in God to bring something good out of them. The most basic and important instruction in all the beatitudes is to trust in God.

In order to read the beatitudes as instruction in "the complete art of happiness" as Wesley suggests, one saying in particular needs to be interpreted carefully for women. The beatitude about the meek often reinforces women's socialization to be quiet, demure, and submissive. Especially if it is taken as an instruction by Jesus for what Christian life should be like, it may prevent women from standing up for themselves or others in situations of injustice, or even danger. What women need to know about this beatitude is that the word *praus* in the original Greek means something quite different than what we think of when the word is translated as "meek." In English, "meek" is often taken to mean "weak." We think of a meek person as a doormat, someone spineless, who gets walked over by everyone else. The Greek word *praus*, however, did not have this connotation. In ordinary speech, it could refer to a wild animal that had been tamed, for instance a horse that could be ridden. It could also refer to a gentle breeze. In both cases, the animal and the wind have great power that is capable of destruction, but this power is used gently. For humans, the Greek word could refer to being tranquil, calm, or composed, especially in difficult circumstances, for instance keeping anger in check. A person who is described in this way is not powerless or weak, but is rather one who has the inner strength to keep from exploding in rage. The one who is blessed, then, is one who has power but keeps it under control. This is not a description of weakness, but rather of gentle strength. Knowing the original meaning of the beatitude, this saying could contribute to instruction about a happy life quite differently than when it is taken to recommend weak submissiveness.

In Luke's gospel, the beatitudes are followed by "woes." Like Deuteronomy, Luke's gospel recognizes that there is a path that leads to flourishing life and a path that leads to death. Luke's concern for social justice is expressed in the way he talks about both blessings and woes. The ones who are blessed are the ones who suffer in this life. Those who have enjoyed pleasure and ease in this world have already had their reward. People who have sought to fulfill their lives through material gain and social status have already experienced the fulfillment they seek, and they will find that it is temporary and easily lost. In contrast, the ones who have been deprived of this temporary and insecure fulfillment will be blessed by God with lasting, secure fulfillment that only God can give, that is, true happiness. Luke's reminder that there are consequences to seeking the wrong kind of happiness is important for understanding what God would have us seek instead.

HAPPINESS IN PAUL'S EPISTLES

Although Paul does not use the term *makarios* for happy or happiness much in his letters, he does talk about rejoicing and being glad and cheerful. His letter to the Philippians especially encourages us to rejoice, as he says in Philippians 4:4, "Rejoice in the Lord always; again I say Rejoice." A reading attributed to Pseudo-Ambrosius reflects on Paul's words with these thoughts:

Beloved brethren, you have heard in the present reading how St. Paul says *I want you to be happy, always happy in the Lord.* For the salvation of our souls God in his goodness calls us to the joys of everlasting blessedness. The joys of this world lead to eternal sorrow; but those who persevere in following the joys that are to be found in the will of the Lord will find themselves led to an enduring, an eternal world. So St. Paul says again, *I repeat, what I want is your happiness.*

He is urging us to grow in the joy that leads to God and to the fulfillment of God's commandments. The more we strive to obey the precepts of our Lord God in this world, the more blessed we shall be in the life to come and the greater will be the glory that we receive in God's presence.[5]

The writer of this commentary on Paul's letter understands Paul to be talking about happiness as blessedness. This is the only true, lasting happiness and this is the happiness Paul wants for the followers of Jesus to whom he is writing. It is also the happiness that even now we as Christians should seek. As the writer points out, other things can lift our spirits temporarily, but they will ultimately let us down. Only happiness in God will sustain us through our entire lives and even in the life to come.

Paul's own life was difficult. He was beaten and imprisoned because of his faith in Jesus Christ. Still, he understands the Christian life to be fundamentally joyful because of what we have received from God through Jesus Christ. To have received salvation, to live in the dominion of grace, to participate in the body of Christ, to expect resurrection—all these are reasons to be glad regardless of our circumstances. If this happiness shapes our life, then all our actions to further God's kingdom on this earth ought to be filled with happiness. This is why Paul tells us that "God loves a cheerful giver" (2 Corinthians 9:7) and instructs those who perform acts of mercy to do so cheerfully (Romans 12:8). In our giving and in our mercy we reflect the grace and mercy of God, so our actions should reflect our happiness in God. Knowing we have received so much, how can we not share with a glad and grateful heart?

THEOLOGIANS INTERPRETING THE BIBLE

Theologians in the early church understood very well that the Bible spoke about our happiness. They also knew that happiness was a topic of concern for philosophers of their time because happiness is so fragile and insecure. Life is uncertain, prosperity and comfort may not last, and this vulnerability led to asking about how to seek lasting happiness. Philosophers answered the question in different ways. Some thought that pleasure was the source of happiness, and even though it was fleeting, one should seek as much pleasure as possible in this life. Others treated the vulnerability of happiness differently. Instead of trying to gain as much as possible, knowing it would not last long, they sought to control their expectations and responses to their circumstances so their happiness would not depend so much on what happens around them. For instance, if you can cultivate a way of thinking that riches are not as important as most people think they are, then losing your possessions would be less damaging to your happiness. This point of view believed happiness in oneself to be more secure than happiness in external things or events. Although these philosophical schools no longer exist formally in our society, these strategies still get used.

Self-mastery of one's emotional responses to the things that happen in life was a widespread value in the ancient world. The dominant philosophy that supported this practice is one that comes to us through Plato and Aristotle. They believed that true happiness is gained by fulfilling our human nature. If you know what a human being is supposed to be, then you can seek those things that will fulfill your nature as a human being. It was believed that as rational creatures, we were most fulfilled when reason was in control of our passions. A person who succeeded in such rational control was considered to live a praiseworthy life.

As Christian theologians interpreted the Bible, they looked to the best wisdom of their time to help them understand what God was saying. They felt free, then, to borrow some ideas about happiness from philosophers, but they did not borrow those ideas without reflecting on them from a Christian point of view. They adjusted those ideas in light of what they learned from scripture. For instance, they learned from philosophers that our deepest fulfillment comes from living according to our nature. However, they learned from the Bible that human nature should be understood as being made in the image of God. So they developed the belief that to be truly happy, our natures made in the image of God must truly reflect God. Such a life is not merely praiseworthy—it is holy. These are the ideas that have shaped the tradition of the church, and they point us to what we need to consider as we think about happiness.

The biblical view, shared and developed further in the Christian tradition, is that happiness is not just lightheartedness, but it is also the deep satisfaction and fulfillment felt by living a life that is pleasing to God. Responding to what God has done for us, a happy Christian takes pleasure in serving God. There is delight and enjoyment in this, but it is not found in simply seeking superficial pleasures or entertainment. It is wise, obedient, and reverent—a life that can be recognized by other humans as well as by God as holy.

CONCLUDING THOUGHTS

Although in recent years, Christians have been reluctant to use the word "happy" to describe their life with God, the Bible does not avoid that word or idea at all. The practice of distinguishing "happiness" from "joy," arose in order to do something important, that is to distinguish true happiness from false happiness. But to use the word "happiness" only for false happiness is misleading when we read translations of the Bible or theologians like John Wesley who use "happy" and "happiness" quite freely when they talk about life with God. In fact, because some English translations of the Bible do use the word "happy" at all, we must think about what is meant by that word.

The Bible gives us much guidance for thinking about happiness if we pay close attention to what it is saying. For many centuries, theologians turned to the Bible to discover what happiness truly is. Their wisdom comes to us as

United Methodists through the theology of John Wesley. The next chapter will look at how Wesley understood the happiness we have in God in connection to the salvation he preached. Because his message about salvation was fundamentally a message about true happiness, he offered something that many in his time and place wanted to hear.

People in our time and place are no less interested in happiness. It is being studied by the social sciences and written about by many people who think they have the key to finding it. If we learn what the Bible and our tradition have to say about happiness, we will have a much better idea of how to think about the many resources in our culture that claim to offer us happiness. We will also have a way to share our faith that people will really want to hear.

ENDNOTES

1. Ellen Charry, *God and the Art of Happiness* (Grand Rapids, Mich.: William. B. Eerdmans Publishing Company, 2010).

2. Ibid., 82.

3. "Martyrdom of Saints Perpetua and Felicitas" in *The Acts of the Christian Martyrs,* trans. and ed. by Herbert Musurillo (Oxford: Oxford University Press, 2000).

4. John Wesley, *Explanatory Notes Upon the New Testament*, http: wesley.nnu.edu/ john-wesley/john-wesleys-notes-on-the-bible/notes-on-the-gospel-according-to-st-matthew/#Chapter+V.

5. Catholic Caucus: Daily Mass Readings, October 6, 2006, www.freerepublic.com/focus/ f-religion/1714938/posts.

CHAPTER 5

John Wesley's Theology of Happiness

By Sarah Heaner Lancaster

The Bible defines a blessed and holy life as a righteous life, one that puts us in right relationship with God because we have followed God's commands and gained wisdom. A righteous life is considered a holy life. Only God is truly holy, but because we are made in the image of God, we reflect God's holiness when our lives are righteous. God evaluates an upright life as good. John Wesley understood "scriptural holiness" as the goal of Christian life, and he connected it with happiness through his understanding of the image of God.

Happiness was so central to Wesley's understanding of salvation that when he wrote in his journal about his heart-warming experience at Aldersgate, he mentioned how "the enemy" tried to make him question his faith by questioning his joy. In response, Wesley came to understand that the "transports of joy" that some feel in conversion experiences do not necessarily come to everyone, and so he characteristically talked about joy as calm and peaceful instead of overwhelmingly intense.[1]

THE IMAGE OF GOD

Christian theologians took the biblical ideas of happiness that were explored in the previous chapter and developed them further. As they thought about how we were made in the image of God they understood that we were made to be in relationship with God—to love and worship God. If human nature is made for this relationship, then human nature is fulfilled by this relationship. The very essence of who we are is fulfilled by our relationship with God. The kind of relationship that fulfills us happens when we love God above everything else. Worshiping God properly means putting God above everything else. To put something else before God is idolatry.

But humans have been affected by sin; as a result we do not desire God above all other things. Instead, we desire things that are less than God. By desiring these other things and seeking to have them, we let those lesser things determine our lives. We look to created things instead of the Creator to fulfill us. This idolatry of other things leads to unhappiness. The lesser things we desire cannot fulfill us, so even when we get them, we are not complete. Our lives are neither holy (God does not evaluate them as upright), nor happy (they are not fully rewarding). The only way we can be truly happy is when we are happy in God.

John Wesley followed in this tradition of thinking about the image of God. He believed that human beings were made to be happy—happy in God. Wesley thought about the image of God in three ways, as natural, political, and moral. The natural image of God is what is in the nature of every human being: to be a spiritual being that has reason, free will, and emotions. The political image refers to how human beings were given some dominion over the rest of creation, so we share in God's governance. The moral image is to reflect God's righteousness and holiness. Sin distorts the moral image of God in us, because our idolatry of other things is unrighteous. Salvation is what God does to restore the moral image in us and make us whole as we were intended to be. Wesley's entire ministry was focused on helping people recover what he called "scriptural holiness."[2]

Although we were made to be happy, we allow our desire for other things to displace God in our lives. When we do so, we cannot be happy. Instead, we are miserable. Wesley built his theology of salvation around this idea. God wants us to be in right relationship not only after we die, but even in this present life. Salvation includes all the things that restore us to the happiness for which we were made in this life. Wesley understood the Bible to say that the way to be happy was to be holy, so he preached holiness and happiness as fundamental to the Christian life. He cared about true happiness in the Christian faith so much that more than eighty of his one hundred fifty collected sermons use the word "happiness."

When Wesley talks about being happy in God, he is not talking about merely feeling lighthearted, nor was he talking about just having fun. He meant a deep contentment and fulfillment that comes from knowing your life is what it is supposed to be. God created us with the desire to live for God, and when that desire is fulfilled by actually living for God, then we are as deeply happy as we can be. Many Methodists who followed the discipline Wesley recommended found this happiness. Ann Gilbert, an early Methodist who dared to preach, wrote, "I have always found that the more diligent I was in using the means of Grace, . . . the more happiness I have enjoyed in my soul."[3] Toward the end of her life, Grace Bennet, an early Methodist leader who worked directly with Wesley wrote:

> My happiest days were when I rose at 4 o'clock for prayer, and preaching at five. And I would say it to the praise and glory of God, I find it no cross at this day (being in my 84th year) to rise early to wait upon God with his people no more than when I was *thirty*.[4]

The happiness these Methodist women were experiencing was the deep, solid, substantial fulfillment that only a relationship with God can bring.

In order to see how happiness and the image of God are connected, it may be helpful to have in mind one use of the word "happy" that is not very common any longer but was used in Wesley's time. The word "happy" could mean fit, suitable, or appropriate. For instance, a "happy thought" or "happy use of language" meant a thought or word especially suited to the occasion.

Even now, we may say a house is "happily situated" when it is well-placed in its surroundings. This use of the word "happy" helps us see how happiness and holiness belong together. For Christians, a happy life, a life that others consider excellent and is also rewarding to the person, is a life that is reflecting God. It fits with the way God wants us to live, so it is well-suited for relationship with God. When our lives fit the way God wants us to be, we are happy in three senses: we have a life that can be evaluated as good and upright, we are personally and deeply satisfied, and we are suited to reflect God. Holiness is an essential component to the full meaning of happiness.

SALVATION AND HAPPINESS

John Wesley understood how essential holiness was to happiness, and he frequently paired the words "holiness" and "happiness" together. For Wesley, holiness was gained by following God's commands, and he used Jesus' summary of the law as the commands that needed to be obeyed: loving God with all your heart, mind, soul, and strength and loving your neighbor as yourself (Mark 12:29–31). Holiness, then, is really about loving well, not simply as a feeling but also as a demonstration of that love in how you live. Wesley talks about both inward and outward holiness. Inward holiness is the love we have in our heart. Outward holiness is the way we show that love in our actions. Inward love in the heart gives rise to outward actions.

Because the root of sin is misdirected desire—desire to be fulfilled by something other than God—our basic problem is that we love poorly. Wesley developed a way of talking about desire that would help us identify and repent of sin. He talked about three main categories of desire: desire of the flesh, desire of the eye, and desire of praise (sometimes called pride of life).[5] The first category, desire of the flesh, includes the ways that we are drawn to things that give us bodily pleasure. This category is especially associated with the senses of taste, touch, and smell. Things in the world that please these senses hold such attraction that they can easily become addictions, but they may also be things that we need for a healthy life (such as food). When

Wesley talked about this category of sin, he did not mean that everything that pleases our body is sinful. Instead, he meant that we could desire things that give us pleasure so much that they could exert power over us. When we think that these things are what we need to be fulfilled as human beings—so that we think we are complete, important, and everything we should be when we have them, or think that something is wrong with us if we do not have them—we have made them into idols. Seeking happiness in them instead of in God is what is sinful.

The second category, desire of the eye, includes things that attract our imaginations. This category is especially associated with the senses of seeing and hearing because we often encounter things that strike our imaginations through watching or listening to them. Whether it is beauty or ideas, we can be drawn to things that are more mentally pleasurable than physically pleasurable. Again, things that please our imaginations are not in themselves sinful. We need stimulation of our minds for a healthy life. But these things, too, can exert power over us if we desire them in the wrong way. Wesley talks about the way we crave novelty and new things that please our imaginations, such as the latest fashion, the latest technological gadget, the most beautiful décor. As with the first category, when we think we need this stimulation to be fulfilled as human beings, we have made them into idols. Seeking happiness in them instead of in God is sinful.

The third category, desire of praise, brings out the danger of how we care what other people think about us. The desire for praise is a major motivator in life, but it can foster pride when we receive it. Not receiving it can lead to self-doubt. We can let what others think of us determine how we feel about ourselves in either of those ways—either by depending on their regard for us to think well of ourselves, or thinking badly of ourselves because we do not have the high regard of others. It is not wrong to consider what others think of us as an important reflection of how we are doing. However, if we think that we are fulfilled, or not fulfilled, because of what others think of us, we have turned human regard into an idol. Seeking happiness in the way other people see us instead of in how God sees us is sinful.

As desires, each of these categories shows how we can be drawn to something in the world more than we are to God, whether it is a material object, an intangible pleasure, or the way we are regarded by those around us. Wesley considered sin to be much deeper than the behaviors that people usually call sins. Those behaviors occur because our desires are already misdirected. Something has gone wrong internally before we commit an outwardly wrong action. For Wesley, the root of our misery is that we do not love as we should. The wholeness that salvation brings in this life is that we become able to love God and neighbor properly. When we have that wholeness, we will know true happiness. Sadly as we saw in Chapter 3, the goal of advertising is often to promise happiness by promoting the desires Wesley warned against, so the product can never deliver on the promise that the advertisement makes.

We need to learn to love well, and grace enables us to do that. In order to direct our love to God above all else, we need to know how much God loves us. Of course, God displayed love for us in Jesus Christ, but we need to know that love as more than an event of the past. We each need to know that God's revelation of love in Jesus Christ is meant for us personally and is available to us now. Wesley believed the Holy Spirit could make God's love in Christ known to each of us individually when we humbly seek it through repentance of our sin. The assurance that we receive from the Holy Spirit that our sins are forgiven is a powerful experience of God's love. Having that love made powerfully known to us draws forth from us our love for God. We are so convinced of God's love for us that we are able to open ourselves to God in a more complete way than ever before and return the love that God deserves. When we know God's love for us so that we are able to love God as we should, we are in truly right relationship with God. Loving God above all else changes us so that we begin to see the world as God sees it. We love what God loves and value what God values. This leads us to loving all those that God loves. Loving neighbor, then, follows directly from loving God. When we love God and neighbor, we are fulfilling God's commands, and so we are holy.

HAPPINESS THROUGH HOLINESS

This kind of love does not happen all at once, though. Because John Wesley thought of salvation not only as what happens to us when we die, he also saw it as a kind of healing in this life. God's forgiveness of our sin opens the way for us to begin to change and become more as God created us to be. The human problem of misdirected desire is quite serious, and it is deeply rooted in us. It takes time and disciplined cooperation with God to redirect our desires to the kind of pure and thorough love for God and neighbor that God wants us to have. So Wesley talks about holiness of heart and life, in other words, holy loving and holy doing. The two are connected and are mutually supporting.

When he talks about holy loving, Wesley uses words that may seem strange to us: tempers and affections. These are words that refer to what we today might call feelings or emotions, or even temperament. Our emotional responses to the things that go on around us reveal what we really think is important. We worry about the things that we care about, and we care about what we think is important. We celebrate when something we think is important happens, and we are sad when something goes wrong with it. Our emotions are good indicators of what we really desire, so they can tell us much about whether we truly love God above other things.

Wesley records in his journal his reaction to reading a theologian whose writing he found to be haughty, overbearing, and opinionated. He found these tempers to be so off-putting that he said if he thought they were how Christians ought to be, he would reject Christianity entirely.[6] Tempers (or temperament) matter because they bear witness to how God is working in our hearts.

Because of this, Wesley asked Methodists to pay attention to what was going on in their emotional lives. Wesley frequently lists the fruits of the Spirit that Paul names in Galatians 5:22–23 as inward qualities to cultivate. They are listed here as he named them in eighteenth-century language and (in parentheses) as they are translated in more modern language in the New Revised

Standard Version (NRSV) of the Bible: love, joy, peace, long-suffering (patience), gentleness (kindness), goodness (generosity), fidelity (faithfulness), meekness (gentleness), and temperance (self-control).

The most basic and important holy tempers for Wesley, though, are gratitude and benevolence, that is, a heart that is grateful to God and that wishes well for others. Whether a person reacts to a bad situation with patience or impatience may well reflect how much gratitude and benevolence a person has. For instance, consider different kinds of reactions to a delayed flight while traveling. A person who is grateful for safety or the ability to travel at all and who wishes well for the other travelers and the airline employees may react quite differently than a person who only thinks about her or his own convenience and schedule. Our gratitude to God reflects our love for God, and our ability to wish others well reflects our love for neighbor. So our tempers and affections reveal how well we obey the central commandments and how closely we reflect the holiness of God.

However important it is, though, inward holiness is not sufficient by itself. Our love must be expressed, so it must lead to outward actions. If we truly love God, we will do things that bring us closer to God. For Wesley, that meant we will make use of the means of grace that God has provided to us to draw us near. He especially recommended prayer, reading, and meditating on scripture, and receiving Holy Communion.[7] Each of these are means that God has provided for growing closer to God, so they should be used by us often. When we do make use of them, we are showing our love for God by devoting time with God. They are expressions of love as well as means of grace. Methodists call these works of piety.

If we truly wish well for our neighbors, then we will actively seek to relieve their distress. Any action that aids our neighbors is an expression of love for them, but Wesley especially encouraged the activities named in Matthew 25:34–36: feeding the hungry, giving drink to the thirsty, welcoming the stranger, clothing the naked, caring for the sick, and visiting those in prison. It is not enough to do no harm to your neighbor. Christ calls us to do something positive for our neighbor. All of these are means of grace as well as expressions of love. Methodists call these things works of mercy.

Works of piety and works of mercy do not save us or by themselves make us holy, but when they are motivated by inward love, they demonstrate holiness. When love is rooted in the heart, it cannot help but send out branches and bear fruit.

As we see the grace of God making a greater and greater difference in our lives, making us more loving and using us for more service, we experience more and more satisfaction and feel more fulfilled, so we are more and more happy. We gain happiness through holiness, through following God's ways, and allowing ourselves to be changed in the process.

John Wesley called this process of becoming more and more holy "sanctification." He understood that we could become really different because of the work of God in our lives, and this difference is just as much what he meant by salvation as going to heaven when we die.[8] We don't just need to be forgiven, or justified, we also need to be renewed in the moral image of God so that we can reflect God's glory and holiness. Only then can we be truly fulfilled. Being happy in God, then, is part of God's saving work in us. This happiness is available to us now if we open ourselves to it, and let God lead us to the life God would have us live.

HAPPINESS AS A FEELING

John Wesley lived in eighteenth-century England, and his ideas were affected by the ideas of his time. Happiness was such an important idea in his time that poets and authors wrote about it. But the understanding of happiness was undergoing some change from what the ancient philosophers and theologians thought about it. Living conditions were improving. The industrial revolution made products more available and less expensive than they had been before, so people could own more things that made their lives easier.

People thought of a happy life as one that had satisfied desires rather than one that was praiseworthy or holy.

This development in eighteenth-century England was one important reason Wesley gave attention to thinking about the kinds of desires people have. Does satisfying our desires really make us happy? Most satisfactions are only temporary. Wesley concluded that the only way to lasting, true happiness is satisfying the desire for God. In thinking like this, Wesley was exercising some criticism of the cultural values in his time. The culture said that happiness was getting what you want. Wesley did not encourage finding happiness simply in getting what you want. He called people to want God above everything else. We have to start with wanting the right thing. He encouraged seeking true happiness in the satisfied desire for God.

It is important to remember that by warning about desire in the way he did, Wesley was not against pleasure. He had to explain himself on this point because this matter is so easy to misunderstand. Enjoying God's creation is part of the happiness for which we are made. But we have to enjoy it as God's creation, as a gift to us for which we should be grateful to God, not as something that alone will fulfill us. So we may enjoy our food or our beds or our devices that make life easier or entertaining, but we must enjoy them as gifts, and we must not let having them or not having them determine our lives or keep us from attending to our relationship with God. Wesley did not rule out pleasure, but he saw a critical difference between taking pleasure in things simply to gain the good feeling they bring and taking pleasure in things as God's good gifts—received gratefully and enjoyed responsibly.

Because so many people around him thought about happiness as pleasure or satisfied desire, Wesley had to explain the kind of happiness he meant very carefully. Although he did not distinguish between happiness and joy, he did make a similar distinction but with different words. He used the word "merry" to talk about lighthearted, frivolous feelings and passing pleasures. He notes that a person can feel merry when they seek worldly desires (a good meal, the latest fashion, a party) and get them, but this satisfied desire is not what he would call happiness. Feeling good in these ways is not fulfillment of our natures as the image of God. The happiness that fulfills us is happiness in God, not in a good meal or a party. Although Christian happiness includes enjoyment and pleasure, it is not defined by those things. It is marked rather by a deep fulfillment in relationship with God. Those enjoyments or pleasures can never be more than temporary, while fulfillment in God is lasting.

Another reason Wesley worried about lightheartedness is that it could often be gained at another person's expense. Methodists in Wesley's time were often mocked by others because they were so disciplined in their lives with God. The name "Methodist" in fact came from teasing about being methodical in their devotional lives. Wesley knew that people attempt to lift their spirits at the expense of others. Ridicule can feel very good to the persons doing the ridiculing, but that way of feeling good does not bring happiness in God. Laughing at another person is hurtful to that person and so is directly contradictory to God's command to love your neighbor. Ridicule cannot bring happiness because it does not make you more holy. Not all lighthearted feelings, then, are genuinely happy feelings. So Wesley's theology of happiness calls us to examine our good feelings to see whether they are bringing us closer to God or separating us from God.

To summarize, the kind of happiness that Wesley means is different from simple lightheartedness as follows: Christian happiness does not exclude fun, but it is not defined by it, and some types of fun are excluded because they distract from or even damage relationship with God and with our neighbors. Enjoyment of life is included in the happiness for which we were made, but we have to be discerning about the kind of enjoyment we take in the things around us.

In eighteenth-century England, it was unseemly for well-bred people to laugh out loud. Laughter was disruptive to social peace, and it showed a loss of control over oneself. As a man of his time and a gentleman, Wesley did not think highly of laughter. This does not mean he was against good humor, but when he thought of happiness as a feeling, he thought of it as calm, peaceful joy instead of boisterous merriment. Today, we are not confined to Wesley's cultural expectations about how we should express our Christian happiness, so laughter can be a healthy way to show the happiness we feel. Still, we should bear in mind his concern not to confuse momentary levity with deep, lasting contentment that comes from loving and trusting God.

HEAVINESS

Lightheartedness was not the only feeling Wesley had to discuss in order to help Methodists understand Christian happiness. He also had to discuss heavyheartedness. Wesley thought the topic important enough to address the relationship between happiness and sadness in a sermon called "Heaviness Through Manifold Temptations."[9] Because he had linked salvation so closely to happiness, he had to give some account of those times when sincere Christians struggle with sorrow. If they felt sad, did that mean something was wrong with their salvation? Wesley uses the term "heaviness" to talk about this problem. He acknowledges that all of us, even the most faithful, will experience heaviness of heart from time to time. Among the things he named that could cause heaviness were struggle with temptation to sin, chronic or acute illness, poverty, and loss of a loved one.[10] All of these are circumstances that are difficult to bear, disrupting the peace of our souls, and they can affect our mood negatively so we do not feel the lightheartedness that many people think of as happiness.

Because true happiness is not simply identified as a pleasant, elevated feeling, Wesley maintains that it is possible to remain happy in God even when we are sorrowful. What he means by that is that our confidence in God need not be lost because we are facing difficult situations. The struggles he named (and others he does not name) can tempt us to turn away from God, to lose our trust and confidence in God, and only focus on our pain. Wesley uses the term "darkness" to talk about the state of a person who gives up on God and loses faith in these troubling times. But heaviness does not have to lead to darkness. Sadness does not necessarily damage faith. In fact, if we turn to

God in those difficult situations, we have an opportunity to grow in faith and find the peace and comfort of God. This peace and comfort is what he means by true happiness in God. Wesley is working out the meaning of Matthew 5:4, "Blessed (happy) are those who mourn, for they will be comforted." Fulfillment in God lasts even through the difficulties of life.

This matter of finding happiness in God even in troubling times was so important that Charles Wesley wrote about it in hymns. Although only a sampling of his work is still in *The United Methodist Hymnal*, one of his hymns, "Thou Hidden Source of Calm Repose" is a good example of how he understood the happiness of God's solace. Verse 2 of this hymn speaks of the comfort and peace God gives to the "happy soul."[11]

Wesley even went beyond talking about specific circumstances that cause heaviness. In his own way, he addressed what we would now refer to as depression. He acknowledges that sometimes sadness can become a "settled temper" lasting for a long time. Even though this feeling may be prolonged, it does not have to become darkness because even in this long sadness Christians may "rejoice." That is, they may be grateful to God, they may enjoy relationship with God, and they may trust that whatever else may be uncertain in their lives, God's love is sure.

Wesley knew that sadness is an inescapable part of life for everyone, and for some it may be prolonged, but because he has not defined happiness as lightheartedness, he can still say that we may be happy in God even when we are sad. In fact, the circumstances that lead to our sadness can also lead to our growth in true happiness if we learn to turn to God in those circumstances. As long as heaviness does not eliminate our faith, hope, and love in God, it does not threaten what Wesley means by happiness, which is not a pleasant, elevated feeling like being merry, but is a deep fulfillment in a relationship. In other words, happiness is the faith, hope, and love we have in God that carries us through those heavy times. No matter how prolonged, if a person is still grateful to God and trusts in God, then sadness does not keep us from being fulfilled in our relationship with God.

CONCLUDING THOUGHTS

It has been observed that we do not always feel happy when we make happiness our goal. If we say "I will be happy," and then constantly monitor our feelings to see if we are happy, we may not be able to meet our own expectations. Furthermore, recent research into happiness shows that people feel happier when they focus on the present than when they focus on the past or future. Although these observations may have a more fleeting feeling than the deep fulfillment Wesley is talking about, they bring out things to think about regarding the way Wesley talks about happiness.

Although he names happiness specifically as a goal for Christian life and faith, Wesley's theology actually directs us to pursue holiness rather than happiness. When he tells Methodists to examine their feelings, he does not tell them to check on their happiness. He tells them to check on their patience, their gentleness, their longsuffering, their humility, and so forth. What we focus on as we live as Christians is to reflect the holiness and righteousness of God in everything we do. For Christians, the freedom we have to pursue happiness is best used in seeking to be holy.

As we look back over our lives, we are able to see how we have grown or where we need to continue to grow. Such self-examination is crucial to Wesley's way of salvation. When we look back and see how God has carried us through difficult times, or how we have made good use of God's grace to respond in a holy way to the irritations of life, then we are able to rejoice in what God has done. When we find areas of our lives that need improvement, we may rejoice that we have a God who offers us forgiveness, and who continually gives us another opportunity to grow.

As important as this self-examination is, it is even more important to focus on what God is doing for us in the present. When Wesley talked about perfection, he meant becoming perfect in love. Because love is what satisfies the commandments of the law, being perfect in love means being holy. Wesley said about perfection (sanctification) that we should expect it in every moment.[12] We should expect that God is able to give us the grace we need to be loving now. In this moment, in this situation, in this action, God can help me to love fully. If we are not expecting God to do so, then there is little chance that we will make use of any grace at all. But if we expect God to give us what we need in every moment to meet every situation, then we will look for God's help and open ourselves to what God would have us do. Our cooperation with God depends on our expectation that God is giving us something to cooperate with. So we must look in every moment for God's work in our lives. Another way to say this is that we must trust God in every moment to be calling forth our response (this trust and response is faith). In this way we are able to increase our love, and as we do so we become more holy. This is what living in the present means for Christian happiness.

Holiness, as we have learned, leads to happiness. The more we open ourselves to God's work in our lives from moment to moment, expecting God to meet us where we are and lead us forward, becoming more loving and holy, the more our lives will reflect the image of God. Our hearts, open to the love of God, will be filled with the love of God for others. A heart that is filled with such love is a happy heart. Not just a temporary good mood, in holiness we find the lasting fulfillment that is true happiness.

ENDNOTES

1. John Wesley, "An Extract of the Rev. John Wesley's Journal from February 1, 1737–38 to His Return from Germany," in *The Works of John Wesley, Volume 18: Journals and Diaries*, ed. by W. Reginald Ward and Richard P. Heitzenrater (Nashville: Abingdon Press, 1988), 250.

2. "Minutes of Several Conversations between the Rev. John Wesley and Others" (London: John Kershaw, 1827), question 3.

3. Paul Wesley Chilcote, *Her Own Story: Autobiographical Portraits of Early Methodist Women* (Nashville: Kingswood Books, 2001), 51.

4. Ibid., 75–76.

5. John Wesley, Sermon 44, "Original Sin," in *The Sermons of John Wesley*, General Board of Global Ministries of The United Methodist Church, www.umcmission.org/ Find-Resources/John-Wesley-Sermons/Sermon-44-Original-Sin, II.9–11. (All of Wesley's sermons may be found on the General Board of Global Ministries website: www.umcmission.org/Find-Resources/John-Wesley-Sermons/Numeric-Index).

6. John Wesley, "Friday, December 26, 1740," in *The Works of John Wesley, Volume 19: Journals and Diaries II*, ed. by W. Reginald Ward and Richard P. Heitzenrater (Nashville: Abingdon Press, 1990), 175–176.

7. John Wesley, Sermon 16, "The Means of Grace," in *The Sermons of John Wesley*, General Board of Global Ministries of The United Methodist Church, www.umcmission.org/ Find-Resources/John-Wesley-Sermons/Sermon-16-The-Means-of-Grace, II.1.

8. John Wesley, Sermon 43, "The Scripture Way of Salvation," in *The Sermons of John Wesley*, General Board of Global Ministries of The United Methodist Church, www. umcmission.org/Find-Resources/John-Wesley-Sermons/Sermon-43-The-Scripture-Way-of-Salvation, I.1.

9. John Wesley, Sermon 47, "Heaviness Through Manifold Temptations," in *The Sermons of John Wesley*, General Board of Global Ministries of The United Methodist Church, www.umcmission.org/Find-Resources/John-Wesley-Sermons/ Sermon-47-Heaviness-Through-Manifold-Temptations.

10. John Wesley, Sermon 47, "Heaviness Through Manifold Temptations," III.2–6.

11. "Thou Hidden Source of Calm Repose," *The United Methodist Hymnal* (Nashville: Abingdon Press, 1989), 153.

12. John Wesley, Sermon 43, "The Scripture Way of Salvation," III.18.

CHAPTER 6

Methodist Practices for Happiness

By Sarah Heaner Lancaster

If the way to gain the happiness that Wesley talked about is to pursue holiness, then how do we do that? How do we regain the moral image of God so that we become who God created us to be? Most people may not think of discipline when they think of happiness, but in the Methodist way of happiness, it takes discipline to pursue the holiness that brings happiness. This chapter will explore some of the practices that Methodists pursued with discipline to grow in the holiness they knew would lead to their happiness in God.

SOCIAL RELIGION

Methodists did not pursue holiness alone, but together. They achieved the discipline needed to pursue holiness by coming together to share their spiritual journeys and hold one another accountable. They did so according to the organizational model envisioned by John Wesley. Wesley always remained a priest in the Church of England, and it was never his intention to separate from that church. Instead, he started a movement within the church to revitalize it and to encourage its members to lead a deeper Christian life. The word used to describe the Methodist organization in the eighteenth century was not "church" but "society," which indicated that people within the Church of England were gathering together apart from ordinary worship times for continued spiritual nourishment. A society does not exist independently of a church, but rather within it and alongside it for the purpose of cultivating greater commitment to the life with God that the church offers. Regular meetings during the week provided Methodists with accountability, means of grace, and personal relationships that all contributed to their growth in holiness.

The organization of Methodism into societies, with even smaller subgroups, went along with Wesley's conviction that Christianity is a social religion. By that he meant that the Christian life called for being in the company of others. As he understood the kind of life God was calling Christians to, many things necessary to that life could not be accomplished alone. Although periods of solitude and private devotion can be helpful at times, they can never replace the way we grow in our life with God when we are with others. We need other people to be able to develop the qualities that mark the life of a Christian. For instance, a fruit of the Spirit we talked about in the previous chapter is patience. There is no better way to practice patience than by being around people who try our patience. We have an opportunity to respond to the irritation we feel by calling upon God to help us respond in a loving way. Learning to be gentle in our responses to others requires having others around. If we want to be peacemakers, then we have to be around people who are in conflict. Only when we are where conflict takes place, or is about to take place, can we provide a calming influence. This certainly does not mean we create conflict in order to calm it, but peacemakers cannot avoid the very situations that call for their presence. Without being around others, even or especially in situations that challenge us, we cannot develop some of the most defining qualities of the Christian life.

One of the main ways that Methodists gained from being in relationship with others in small groups outside of regular worship was that these relationships allowed them to be honest with themselves and with each other about the ways God was working in their lives and about what still needed to be healed by grace. They were expected to share with each other about the state of their souls and receive encouragement or admonition from others in the group. Such open sharing depended on serious pursuit of holiness, but it also resulted in lives that were indeed happy in God. In the eighteenth century, Methodist John Murlin wrote, "I now met with my class constantly, to whom I sometimes gave a word of exhortation. And I never found myself more happy than when I was among the children of God."[1] These meetings never replaced worship in the church, but they provided a level of honest relationship on a regular basis that ensured that Christianity was for Methodists a truly social religion.

Now that Methodism has become a church, it needs to find a way to help its members gain the benefits of the social religion that Wesley made available through the societies. Isolated Christians miss out on many of the benefits that Methodism has to give, and the larger congregations are, the more likely it is that isolation will occur. Churches should encourage small groups and other forms of interaction, not just for fun, but for disciplined pursuit of holiness. United Methodist Women circles present prime opportunities for such meaningful relationships. Although we saw in Chapter 2 how important friends are to our happiness and well-being, Wesley challenges us to do more than take refuge in our comfortable relationships.

We need other people not only to grow in our inner spiritual lives, but also in order for our faith to express itself in works. As we saw in the previous chapter, loving neighbor as we love ourselves leads us to perform works of mercy. Because a faith that does not express itself in works is dead, these works are absolutely central to a faithful Christian life. To serve Jesus in the form of our neighbor, as Matthew 25:31–46 describes, we must know real people who are in need and respond to those needs. The care that we express toward others, whether friend or stranger, is essential to living out the faith we profess.

The social nature of Christian faith is especially well expressed in Wesley's sermon "On Visiting the Sick."[2] In it, he explored one of the forms of care listed in Matthew 25:35–36, taking care of the sick, to provide instruction on how we are to be employed in the work of God. Wesley's insights about visiting the sick may be extended to other works of mercy. In this sermon, Wesley informs us that works of mercy, like works of piety, are means of grace. By this he meant that we may receive God's grace through them, so they are vehicles for us to grow in grace. Like works of piety, then, they should be undertaken often. They are crucial instruments that God has given to us for helping us along the way of salvation.

Not only are works of mercy a means that God makes available to us to grow in grace, they are also a duty. We cannot neglect them, then, if we want to remain upright in our relationship with God. In fact, it is plain in Matthew 25:31–46 that just as performing this duty leads to life with God, the consequence of leaving this duty unperformed is to be cut off from life with God. Therefore, Wesley lamented how often even those who claim to love God ignore this duty. So he writes this sermon in order to explain the duty and to encourage more to attend to it.

By "the sick," Wesley did not mean only those who are physically ill.[3] He also included people who are sick at heart, in other words, those who are afflicted in spirit as well as in body. Whether their illness is physical or mental and emotional, they are in need of care, and the care that we extend to them is care extended to Christ.

By "visiting" Wesley meant seeing the sick in person, actually being present with them.[4] Because he knew that many people want to send aid through someone else rather than take it themselves, he points out that no proxy can perform our duty for us. Although the sick benefit from aid no matter who delivers it, we cut ourselves off from our own spiritual benefit if we are not the deliverers. A substitute cannot discharge the responsibility given directly to us, so even if someone else gives the care, our own duty has not been carried out. Furthermore, he said that by depending on a substitute, we deprive ourselves of a means of grace. It is when we provide care in person that we have the opportunity to be touched by another, to increase our sympathy for those in need and therefore expand our love for our neighbors. We also will likely grow in humility and patience, and other fruits of the spirit, as we deal with the difficulty of the situation. Because Wesley assumed in his context that it was the poor who would especially need visitors to care for them in illness, he observes that much hardheartedness toward the poor is rooted in lack of personal knowledge of them. This insight could be extended to other groups, such as those who suffer from illness with social stigma or people who are heartsick in prison. Wesley decried lack of sympathy born of our "voluntary ignorance" because we do not bother to get to know them. Visiting is a duty Christ has given us in order to open our hearts to love. Finally, visiting in person allows us the opportunity to share the good news of Jesus Christ with the person.

Wesley countered many excuses that people could make to keep from visiting. No one was too important to go. No one was too unskilled in medical care—they could always care for the soul of the person. The young and the old alike could lift a person's spirits. In his time, it was necessary to make the point that even women could perform this service. No one was without some resource to be able to provide some assistance. In fact, he made only one exception for someone not to perform this duty: if the person was him- or herself too sick to go.[5]

Although much good in the world can be done by giving money to others to carry out mission on our behalf, Wesley reminded us that if we want to grow in holiness so that we may have true happiness in God, we must personally engage in works of mercy.[6] If the spirit of God is at work in you, then you have something to share. The very act of arranging a busy schedule to be present with someone in need—whether sick, or in prison, or hungry—allows us to grow in humility, patience, and other fruit that show how the Holy Spirit is working in us. Even if we lack skills for physical care (or doing repairs, or tutoring, or whatever the job), we have something to contribute by doing a work of mercy. A church that wants to enable its members to have the happiness for which we were made will provide broad opportunities for these works and will encourage everyone to participate in them so that their hearts may be enlarged for the needs of the world, and so that they may personally serve Jesus by serving those in need. The mission opportunities provided by United Methodist Women offer a powerful way to embrace the spiritual growth Wesley described.

SPIRITUAL RESPIRATION

In Wesley's theology, growing in holiness is called "sanctification." Wesley described the beginning of this process as a birth. Once we know we have been forgiven (justified), we come into a new life like an infant emerging from the womb. Just as an infant has eyes and ears in the womb, but they cannot yet function very well, we have what Wesley calls "spiritual senses" that enable us to know God, but they do not function very well until we know the love and forgiveness of God. When the Holy Spirit lets us know how much God loves us, all our spiritual senses become activated. We can see and hear God more clearly than ever. We taste the goodness of God. Although God has always been there, we are now in touch with God in a way that allows us to grow and flourish spiritually.

Wesley expanded on this image to describe how we begin to take in God the way a baby's lungs begin to take in air. Although God has always been all around us, we can now breathe deeply and take in the presence that we so thoroughly depend on for life. Our need to breathe in that presence to stay alive spiritually is as great as a baby's need to breathe in air to stay alive physically. Wesley calls this ongoing activity "spiritual respiration."

He described this process as receiving the Spirit (or breath) of God by faith, and then returning that breath by prayer, praise, and thanksgiving. God breathes grace into us, and we breathe our prayer and praise back to God. As long as this cycle of inhaling and exhaling continues, our spiritual life flourishes. We grow and thrive, and we know the wholeness of salvation. Unlike physical respiration, though, we have no involuntary mechanism to keep breathing God's Spirit at all times. Spiritual respiration continues only when we are attentive to maintaining it. God has given us means of grace to help us keep breathing God. The disciplined life that Methodists led focused on consciously taking in the presence of God and returning thanks and praise.

Of course, works of mercy as means of grace are beneficial for this purpose. When we are mindful of performing those duties with and for God, they are life-giving rather than burdensome. Our hearts become more loving, the Holy Spirit shapes even our feelings into the fruit of the Spirit; our awareness of the way that God is using us to improve the situation of another makes us grateful. The relationships that we build with persons around us also build our relationship with God. We miss these benefits when we neglect works of mercy, and eventually our soul will suffocate without them.

Even more clearly directed to cultivating our relationship and dependence on God are works of piety. Wesley ordinarily named these means of grace as searching scripture (hearing, reading, and meditating), public and private prayer, and receiving the Lord's Supper (he also sometimes includes fasting).[7] Each of these activities serves the purpose of drawing us closer to God so that we may be shaped by the power and presence of God that we encounter through them. Using these means of grace regularly and in a disciplined way keeps us focused on our spiritual life so we keep breathing God. These means of grace provide us with both personal and corporate opportunities for growth.

Wesley said these are the ordinary channels that God provides for us to receive grace, so we should not neglect them. To do so puts us at risk to stop breathing God as we should. These, of course, are not the only means God may use, but because God has established them for our benefit, we should use them regularly.

The disciplined life to which Methodists aspired seemed at times a bit fanatical to others, hence the nickname "Methodist." But when Wesley wrote about the distinguishing marks of a Methodist in "The Character of a Methodist," he identified Methodists, not by being methodical or by any doctrines or particular practices, but by their love for God, which made them "Happy in God, yea, always happy, as having in him a 'well of water springing up into everlasting life,' and overflowing his soul with peace and joy."[8] Methodists were those who had a heart that beat for God, so that their very lives were prayers and living sacrifices to God. It was the disciplined spiritual practice that formed them so deeply and so well. Although disciplined in a way others did not always understand, Methodists found what they were looking for, namely, the holiness that gave them happiness.

Too often, Christians rely only on Sunday morning worship as their primary spiritual resource. The heritage of the Methodist tradition calls us to cultivate our life with God continually. The Bible studies provided by United Methodist Women in **response** magazine are an important resource for this. Alone or in groups, we should make regular use of the means God has given us to live in the presence of God. A church that cares about its members' happiness in God will teach them to value and use the means of grace that are works of piety. Without them we risk spiritual suffocation.

SINGING

When Methodists gathered, they sang, and the hymns that Charles Wesley wrote for Methodists helped them maintain their disciplined lives by teaching them the faith, describing the goal they sought, and encouraging them to pursue it. What they learned through verse, they could memorize easily and carry with them in their hearts—always available when they needed it. The verses that the Wesleys published were available also for reading and meditating in times of personal devotion. Because Charles Wesley often wrote in verse form the theology his brother John preached, Methodists had at their disposal resources for learning that could assist in the deep internalization of the most important themes of the Methodist way of salvation.

Whether sung or read as poetry, Charles Wesley's words kept before the Methodists the expectation of being happy in God:

> Still, O my soul, prolong,
> The never-ceasing song! Christ my theme, my hope, my joy;
> His be all my happy days, Praise my every hour employ,
> Every breath be spent in praise.[9]

As the people breathe together in song, the constancy of returning praise in spiritual respiration is reinforced in singing. Just as singing while traveling makes the journey easier, singing hymns of faith carries us along the way of salvation.

Charles Wesley wrote a hymn on the beatitudes that supported John's claim that these verses instructed us in the art of happiness. He describes the way of salvation, beginning with atonement: "Happy soul, from guilt set free, Jesus died for thee, for thee!" As he writes of sanctification, he shows how happiness is tied to holiness of heart:

> Happy soul, as silver tried,
> Silver seven times purified,
> Love hath broke the rock of stone,
> All thy hardness melted down,
> Wrath, and pride, and hatred cease,
> All thy heart is gentleness.

He expresses the renewal of the image of God as renewal in love:

> Happy soul, who now renewed,
> God in thee, and thou in God,
> Only feel'st within thee move
> Tenderness, compassion, love,
> Love immense, and unconfined,
> Love to all of humankind,
> Love, which willeth all should live,
> Love, which all to all would give,
> Love, that over all prevails,
> Love, that never, never fails,
> Stand secure, for thou shalt prove,
> All th' eternity of love.[10]

Several other references to being happy are found in this hymn. As Methodists sang or read descriptions such as these of the life to which they were called, they would be inspired to aspire to holiness so they could find their happiness in God.

In the same collection of hymns, Charles Wesley used the word "happy" in hymns that he wrote for the following occasions: in thanksgiving, desiring to love, in penitence, on a birthday, in pain, for a sick friend, for a preacher, after preaching, when called to give testimony, and even in dying or at the death of a child. The range of situations—from mundane to devastating—to which Charles Wesley could link being happy in God was quite broad. Through these hymns, Methodists were being reminded that they could find happiness in God's presence and work in every event of their lives. They were taught to be attentive to God at all times, and to give praise and thanks constantly. These are the things needed for spiritual respiration.

From Charles Wesley's hymns, Methodists learned how to be happy in God even in sadness. As mentioned in the previous chapter, one of these hymns that communicated this possibility is "Thou Hidden Source of Calm Repose." Read or sung in time of trouble, this hymn offers a vision of finding peace and joy in God, even when hearts are heavy, "in grief my joy unspeakable."[11] Through poetry that speaks about our happiness in sorrow, Methodists turned to God in hope for the comfort and peace that God has promised. Because they turned to God, they received what God had to offer in those difficult times.

Not only the content, but also the way the hymns were sung aided Methodists in their pursuit of holiness and happiness. The last of John Wesley's "Directions for Singing" (number VII, to "sing spiritually") placed at the front of *The United Methodist Hymnal* [12] shows that he saw singing as a spiritual practice. He also wrote that hymns should be sung with energy so they can "awake and enliven the soul."[13] With singing, Methodist discipline and education through verse was not a burden but a spirited joy. The manner in which we sing not only shows that we want to be happy in God, but it also energizes us to hope for what God can do in our lives.

Churches should not ignore the importance of singing our faith—not only to praise, but also, like the psalms, to give voice to the entire scope of the ways God is with us in our complex and messy lives. The psalms attest to the importance of lifting our voices to God. Shared musical experiences add to communal spirituality, and breathing together in singing with others has been known to produce physical effects such as synchronized heart rate.[14] United Methodist Women gatherings often provide an opportunity to share this Methodist tradition of singing. Whether musically gifted or not, all of us can use singing as a spiritual practice. We should not allow either attention to technique or making mistakes to detract from the devotion of making an offering of the heart to God in song.

EXPECTING PERFECTION

One of the hallmarks of early Methodism was its expectation of Christian perfection. John Wesley explained that perfection was another word for holiness,[15] and that both words referred to loving God with your whole heart and your neighbor as yourself. Because he was so often misunderstood when he talked about perfection, Wesley had to spend considerable time and effort explaining it. He knew it was important for people to know what he did not mean by Christian perfection. His list of what it is not corrected some common misunderstandings. First, being perfect as a Christian does not mean being free from ignorance. There will always be things we do not know. Second, because we will not have perfect knowledge, we will never be free from mistakes. Christians seeking perfection can make as many mistakes as other finite human beings. Third, Christian perfection does not mean being free from infirmities—including both physical and mental conditions. Christian perfection does not mean getting healthier or smarter. Fourth, being perfect in love never frees us from the possibility of temptation. There will always be things in the world that will try to draw our love away from God.

The only thing that the Methodist doctrine of perfection is about is love. Wesley realized that Jesus gave us a clear command in the Sermon on the

Mount, "Be perfect, therefore, as your heavenly Father is perfect" (Matthew 5:48). This command follows Jesus' teaching about loving your enemies, so Wesley took the command about being perfect as a command about love. If we are to be perfect as God is perfect, we are to love as God loves.

As we have seen, Wesley understood salvation as something we could know in this life, so Wesley preached that we should expect to be made perfect in love in this life. Whether or not finite human beings can ever fully love with the capacity that God loves, the expectation of loving more and more the way that God loves is important to our pursuit of holiness, and therefore to our happiness in God, because it sets the goal for our life and faith. Wesley denied that we could ever reach an upper limit for love—it could always grow, so we could always expect more. And the expectation of loving more perfectly as God loves is what propels us to grow toward the goodness of God. The hope that we have to become more and more holy (loving) is what drives us to employ all the means of grace that God has provided for us to become more loving. Without that expectation and hope, it is hard to maintain the disciplined life that is called for to pursue holiness. In fact, where he saw a decline in the power and numbers of a Methodist society, Wesley attributed it to a lack of this expectation.

If our happiness in God is related to our holiness, then the expectation to be made more and more loving is crucial to our happiness. Churches need to encourage members to expect to be made really different through their relationship with God. In a Methodist understanding, the hope of being happy in God lies in the expectation of the renewal of the image of God in love. The more we give ourselves to God to help us be more loving, the more God will do so. The more loving we become, the more loving we want to be. As we breathe the love and presence of God more deeply, our hearts grow more full. We cannot help but find our happiness in God with this as our focus. Without this focus, we cannot help but follow our own desires for other things and move farther from the relationship that brings us true happiness. To expect to be made perfect in love, then, sets the course for our journey and fuels our work.

CONCLUDING THOUGHTS

The practices that early Methodists engaged in under John Wesley's guidance led to their happiness in God. They had what many today refer to as life satisfaction. Their lives had meaning and purpose. They could see that their lives were good, and they knew that God considered them to be upright and holy and useful to others. They also knew they were committed and contributing to the everlasting purpose of God. The framework in which they found their meaning was noble and secure. Many (like Ann Gilbert and Grace Bennett in the previous chapter) recorded in journals the happiness they found in the discipline they followed as Methodists. This calm, steady purpose carried them through turbulent and difficult times.

Relationship is an important ingredient of happiness, and the way that Wesley understood and encouraged social religion ensured that Methodists would have and nurture deep relationships with one another and with God. As long as Christians enact social religion, the threat of loneliness need not destroy happiness.

It has been observed that often the happiness one has in pursuing a goal is just as great as the happiness one has in achieving that goal. The expectation of being made perfect in love set for Methodists a goal that could be eternally pursued. It was never finished because love could always grow. Even something less than entire sanctification brought the satisfaction and healing of a more loving heart.

Discipline and accountability may not be the first things that come to mind when thinking about a happy life, but in the early Methodist movement they are the very things that led to the happiness that Methodists actually experienced. Without the same structure that organized the Methodist societies, it will take imagination and creativity to make the Methodist way of happiness available to people once again. But with so much in our heritage to draw from, The United Methodist Church could offer much happiness to the world. United Methodist Women already provides many opportunities to help women participate in the happiness our tradition has to offer, and it could be key to reviving this goal for the whole church.

ENDNOTES

1. John Murlin, "The Life of John Murlin," in *The Lives of Early Methodist Preachers, Chiefly Written by Themselves*, ed. by Thomas Jackson, vol. 3 (London: John Mason, 1837), 417–418.

2. John Wesley, Sermon 98, "On Visiting the Sick," in *The Sermons of John Wesley*, General Board of Global Ministries of The United Methodist Church, www.umcmission.org/Find-Resources/John-Wesley-Sermons/Sermon-98-On-Visiting-the-Sick.

3. Ibid.

4. Ibid.

5. Ibid.

6. Ibid.

7. John Wesley, Sermon 16, "The Means of Grace," in *The Sermons of John Wesley*, General Board of Global Ministries of The United Methodist Church, www.umcmission.org/Find-Resources/John-Wesley-Sermons/Sermon-16-The-Means-of-Grace.

8. John Wesley, "The Character of a Methodist," www.umcmission.org/Find-Resources/John-Wesley-Sermons/The-Wesleys-and-Their-Times/The-Character-of-a-Methodist, 6.

9. Charles Wesley, "3rd Hymn to Christ," verse 1, in *Hymns and Sacred Poems* (1739), ed. John Wesley and Charles Wesley (London: Strahan, 1739), https://divinity.duke.edu/sites/divinity.duke.edu/files/documents/cswt/04_Hymns_and_Sacred_Poems_%281739%29_mod.pdf, 170.

10. Charles Wesley, "The Beatitudes: Matt 5: 3-12," Hymn 8, verses 4, 7, and 9, in *Hymns and Sacred Poems* (1749), vol. 1, ed. Charles Wesley (Bristol: Farley, 1749), 35–40. Accessed in Charles Wesley's Published Verse, Duke Center for Studies in the Wesleyan Tradition.

11. "Thou Hidden Source of Calm Repose," *The United Methodist Hymnal* (Nashville: Abingdon Press, 1989), 153.

12. "Directions for Singing," *The United Methodist Hymnal* (Nashville: Abingdon Press, 1989), vii.

13. John Wesley, "Reasons Against a Separation from the Church of England," in *The Methodist Societies: History, Nature, and Design*, ed. Rupert E. Davies, in *The Works of John Wesley*, volume 9 (Nashville: Abingdon Press, 1989), 340.

14. Björn Vickhoff, et al., "Music Structure Determines Heart Rate Variability of Singers," in *Frontiers in Psychology* 4 (July 2013): 1–16.

15. John Wesley, Sermon 40, "Christian Perfection," in *The Sermons of John Wesley*, General Board of Global Ministries of The United Methodist Church, www.umcmission.org/Find-Resources/John-Wesley-Sermons/Sermon-40-Christian-Perfection, I.9.

CHAPTER 7

Happiness in Simple Living

By Sarah Heaner Lancaster

Disciplined behavior of the kind discussed in the previous chapter leads to holiness of heart, which in turn leads to more holiness of life. Disciplined living requires simple (but not easy) living, and one important area for disciplined, simple living is properly handling money. This is an area of life in which Methodists eventually disappointed John Wesley. It was and continues to be a difficult subject, with fewer embodying holiness in this area than Wesley had hoped. Because so many people assume a direct link between money and happiness, and because Wesley wrote a good bit about this perceived link, this area deserves careful reflection.

SERVING TWO MASTERS

Many Biblical commentators of Wesley's time produced interpretations of the Sermon on the Mount as key instruction about the Christian life. Wesley took his place in this tradition by publishing thirteen sermons on Matthew 5–7. The sermons cover many topics, and they do not present a single, integrated argument, but they all illustrate the implications of saving faith for Christian living. We have already seen that Wesley understood the beatitudes (in Matthew 5) as instruction in the art of happiness, and these thirteen sermons tell us more about practicing this art.

Sermons number eight and nine on the Sermon on the Mount, which together cover Matthew 6:19–34, give Wesley's understanding of what Jesus had to say about money.[1] He roots his reflection in the observation Jesus makes that no one can serve two masters (Matthew 6:24). The two masters between whom we must choose are God and "mammon," as it is described in the King James Version of the Bible. Wesley explained that mammon was the god who ruled over riches, and he further explained that "riches" include not only money, but also everything that can be purchased with money—not just goods, but also comfort, respect, and pleasure.[2] One of the reasons money becomes so important to us is because it gives us access to those things that we want. So Wesley addressed both the attraction of money and the attraction of the things we gain with money.

Because the matter about which Jesus speaks is serving God and mammon, we must understand what it means to "serve" them so we know when and how we are doing so. Wesley understood serving God as believing in God, which for Wesley was not merely an intellectual assent to God's existence or to the things God says. Rather, for Wesley to believe meant three fundamental ways we relate to God: trusting, loving, and resembling.[3] And because believing is serving, these are the three ways we serve God.

To trust in God means to recognize our dependence on God for our strength, our help, and our happiness. In other words, we know that our power comes from God, so we know that we will be sustained by God in any time of trouble, and therefore we may rest and be satisfied in God. Being happy in God, then, is not a reward or something extra in our lives. It is actually a fundamental component of our trust and belief in God. To serve God in this way means that we are mindful of God in everything that we do, that we use the things that God has given us in a way that pleases God, so we enjoy them to bring about God's enjoyment of us.

To love God as service to God means to love God with everything that we are: heart, soul, mind, and strength. It also means to desire God above all else and to desire God for God's own sake, not for what we think we may get from

God. Desiring God above all else does not eliminate desiring other things, but they are desired in connection to God, for instance, they are recognized as gifts from God, or sought in order to serve God, or used to glorify God. This is the only way to desire things without placing them in competition with God. When we always keep God as the focus, then we are able to rejoice and delight in God in everything we do. Living in this way makes it possible for us to be always happy in God.

To resemble God means that we must conform our spirits to the Spirit of God. When we worship, we are not only praising God; we are also performing acts that transform us. The ritual acts in worship help us to gain the mind of Christ so that we will love as God loves, and our spirits will reflect the gentleness, kindness, mercy, compassion, and goodness of God's own Spirit. When we have conformed ourselves to God in this way, then our bodies will also obey, keeping the commandments and doing those works God gives us to do so that we are truly living sacrifices to God.

Once we understand that this is what it means to serve God, then we can begin to understand what it means to serve mammon instead of God. Service to mammon also means trusting, loving, and resembling. We trust in mammon when we think our riches (not only money but also what can be bought with money) give us strength and help and happiness. We take them to be what gives us power, or what will keep us out of trouble, or what gives our lives satisfaction and meaning. If we take riches to have this kind of significance for our lives, then we cannot help but seek more wealth, which we expect to give us more power, more help, and more happiness. And in seeking this in the world rather than in God, we have displaced God as the one in whom we trust.

We love mammon when we desire the things of the world for their own sake instead of for the sake of God. We give our hearts, minds, souls, and strength in pursuit of riches. We give our whole selves to gaining riches so that this is our primary task. Our lives are oriented to gaining more comfort, more worldly respect, more pleasure, and we may pay little attention to the comfort, respect, and pleasure of others in order to get what we want. In directing ourselves to satisfy the desires that riches create for us, we have displaced God as the one we love above all.

We resemble mammon when we conform ourselves to the thinking, expectations, attitudes, values, and customs of a world that has no concern for the Spirit of God. When we let trends, fashion, and ruthless advancement determine our thinking and behavior, we place ourselves above others. When our main focus is our own gain, then we become less concerned about the effects of our lives on others. Our spirits bear the fruits of impatience, harshness, vengeance, competition, and condescension instead of the fruit of the Spirit of God. When we allow ourselves to be shaped by the attitudes and actions of those who care nothing for God, we have displaced God as the measure and model for our lives.

If we want true happiness, we must be true to the true God who gives us happiness. Simple living means remembering there is only one to whom we owe our loyalty. The temptation will always be to try to divide our loyalty, but when we do so, we lose the genuine happiness that we seek. Enjoying the comfort and pleasure that God gives us in the things God has provided for us is quite different from seeking happiness in those things by themselves without regard for God. Confusing the source of our happiness also leads to serious consequences for our formation as human beings—whether we will take on the qualities that the Holy Spirit has to offer, or whether we will take on the qualities of a self-serving world. Remaining loyal to the one we serve makes all the difference.

HAVING A SINGLE EYE

Because of the impossibility of serving two masters, Wesley often talked about having a "single eye." This phrase directs us to keep our focus on God so that we are consciously attentive to God in all that we say and do. If we are constantly directing ourselves toward God as the measure and model for our lives, then we are opening ourselves to be renewed in the image of God. Such intentionality will enable us to serve God above everything else, and to enjoy everything else in a way that is pleasing to God. Having a single eye gives us direction and opportunity for growth in holiness. It also ensures that we are seeking our happiness only in God.

Wesley understood Jesus to be referring to the single eye in the Sermon on the Mount when he instructed us not to store up treasures on earth for ourselves, but rather to store them up in heaven (Matthew 6:19–21). This instruction is important for having a single eye because our hearts will be directed to wherever our treasure is. If we have not accumulated wealth in the world, then we will be less likely to trust in it, love it, and try to find our happiness in it.

Wesley was practical enough to realize that we have to survive in the world, which includes participating in the economic system, so he explained how we might do so without violating Jesus' command not to "store up for yourselves treasures" (Matthew 6:19). Jesus' command permits us to pay our own way, so we do not become indebted to someone else. We are permitted to provide what we truly need for ourselves—food, clothing, shelter, etc. We are not only permitted, but obligated to provide for our dependents—again what they truly need, but not items of luxury or idleness that Wesley called "superfluities."[4] Finally, Wesley understood there are periods when we must put aside money for a later necessary expenditure, and he did not include such saving as storing up treasures. Jesus' instruction is not intended to hinder our living, it is intended rather to keep us from serving another master. Accumulation beyond what we really need as well as hoarding things that could be used to fill another person's need are problems that hurt our souls as well as our neighbors.

Jesus' instruction regarding not worrying about tomorrow (Matthew 6:25–34) is another way of helping us to keep a single eye. Wesley explained that these words do not mean you should not care about anything.[5] In order to provide for our dependents and ourselves, we do need to pay attention to what is going on. We even have to plan, often beyond the current day. This kind of care is necessary for performing our duties to ourselves and to one another. Wesley explained that what Jesus is cautioning against is anxiety about the future. If we have a single eye, we will take care of what is within our power and then leave the rest to God. Anxiety about the future keeps us from enjoying the present moment as God's good gift. Not caring about tomorrow does not eliminate planning, but it allows us to look at what God has done for us today and say, "It is enough."

Having a single eye means keeping our focus always on the one from whom all our strength, help, and happiness come. Shifting that focus away from God leads us into disloyalty to the one we should serve. Accumulating resources beyond what we truly need or worrying about resources beyond our present need both shift our focus off of God and so pose temptations to such disloyalty. The single eye will look to what God is doing for us now and trust in what God will do for us in the future. The happiness of simple living includes keeping a single focus on God, so it has no need to seek happiness in anything else. The simplicity of the single eye helps us be content, a major component of being happy.

THE USE OF MONEY

Despite his warning against serving mammon, Wesley did not understand money in itself to be sinful. In fact, he knew the good it could do in the world. So he did not summon Methodists to poverty. Instead, he tried to give them guidance about how to deal with money so that it would not be a barrier to holiness and instead be employed for God's purposes. Many are familiar with the framework of Wesley's instructions: gain all you can, save all you can, give all you can.[6] Not as many know how he explained the way to carry out each of these directions with holiness.

Gaining all you can is a rule even the ungodly understand, and Wesley could approve of the general concern of the world not to overspend for what one tries to gain. He went much further, though, in pointing out many limitations on how money should be gained. A person should never try to gain money at the expense of his or her life or health. Because life and health are more important than riches, a person should avoid gaining by means of dangerous employment. Wesley was not only concerned about the body but also the mind. Employment that could lead a person into a sinful state of mind, for instance requiring them to cheat or lie, should not be entered into for gain. Some jobs may hurt everyone in this way, while others may be harmful only to individuals with specific weaknesses.[7]

Concern about neighbor also sets some limits on how to gain money. Businesses that hurt another person's ability to do business, or that grow by taking over another person's substance are ruled out. Additionally, one should not be involved in business that hurts others in their lives, health, or soul. So Wesley's first instruction must be understood as gain all you can through honest, safe, wholesome employment. It is not an authorization to make money by any means possible.

Wesley's second instruction, to save all you can, was directed primarily to not gratifying the desires that lead us into sin (of the flesh, eye, or praise). If money is readily available, then these desires can more easily be satisfied, and we will be quite tempted to find our happiness in these gratifications. For this reason, it takes great discipline to follow this instruction. The point is not to save to accumulate more, but rather to avoid spending money on those things that lead you away from God. Wesley calls us to avoid buying things for immediate physical pleasure rather than to meet plain need, buying things for ornamentation rather than necessity, or buying things that will raise our status in the eyes of others. He was not against paying a little more to buy items of high quality if the reason for doing so was that they would last longer and so reduce the expense of replacing them, but this reason is quite different from buying for indulgence or show. The discipline of avoiding waste and of weighing desires against real needs is the heart of this second rule. The simple living that results from measuring one's spending with the single eye of desire for God above all else leads to being satisfied and happy in God.

Although exploitation of labor was known in Wesley's time, it has taken on global proportions that Wesley may not have been able to imagine. If he had thought about such exploitation, his second instruction would no doubt have included concern about buying things at a reduced cost when the laborers were not paid a fair wage. Operating under the principle of the first rule that we are not to hurt our neighbors, it is permissible to pay a little more so that others may have what they need to live.

Under this second instruction, Wesley cautioned against indulging children. Because the ability to make purchases opens the door to gratifying desires, parents can easily be leading their children into sin by buying them things beyond what they need. Children can come to expect that those desires should be gratified, so they are not learning to look to God instead of to things of the world for their happiness. Wesley even takes this concern to the point of saying that saving in order to leave an inheritance could be a danger to the souls of one's heirs. Of course provision should be made for dependents to keep them from want, but all the rest should be used for the glory of God rather than for maintaining a lavish lifestyle.

If Wesley's thoughts about saving seem extreme, it may be helpful to realize he had a personal experience that shaped his thinking. He encountered a young girl who did not have adequate clothing to keep her warm in the cold. Being moved to help her, he reached into his pocket for money but had very little because he had just bought some artwork to hang on the walls of his room. He then realized the direct correlation between his spending on himself for something pleasing but unnecessary, and his inability to help this young girl with what she really needed.[8] What he tried to accomplish in this second rule was to help others make this connection so they may avoid waste and not miss opportunities to take care of genuine need.

The third rule speaks directly to the idea of glorifying God with one's financial resources: give all you can. Even here there are limitations. The genuine needs of oneself and one's dependents must be provided for, so giving stops short of taking from them what they must have to live. The fundamental basis for giving all you can is that nothing that you have gained truly belongs to you, but rather to God. You have merely been given temporary responsibility for it. To care for God's bounty responsibly, you must first provide for yourself and those who depend on you, then you must use all the rest to take care of the needs of others. Wesley called for testing every expense by reflecting on whether you are acting as an obedient steward of God, offering your spending as a sacrifice with which God would be well pleased.[9]

Wesley truly believed that a simple life that followed these rules would be a happy life. Although he took his own rules very seriously, most Methodists in his day stopped short of giving away their entire accumulated surplus. Toward the end of his life, Wesley wrote a sermon to Methodists called "The Danger of Riches," in which he pointed out quite explicitly how surplus opens the way for desires to lead us away from happiness in God and how getting what we want makes us less humble and gentle and patient toward others.[10] Riches, then, harm us in the very areas of our lives that God is trying to make whole. As difficult as it is to follow his rules for the use of money, the consequence of not trying to follow them is costly.

Wesley's high expectation for Methodists to give all that they could was not met. Near the end of his life, Wesley wrote again on this topic in his sermon "On the Danger of Increasing Riches."[11] This was the last sermon he published in the *Arminian Magazine*. The three rules that Wesley outlined for the use of money may not have been observed as fully and precisely as he had hoped, but members of The United Methodist Church may still learn from him about how to have a simpler, holier, and happier life. Wesley never stopped calling Methodists to give everything beyond what they truly needed. In addition to these three rules, he also left a sliding scale to help evaluate the use of money.

SCALE FOR SIMPLIFYING

By the time he wrote about the danger of riches, Wesley was using language that offered some flexible guidance for how to follow the rules he tried to establish. Wesleyan scholar Richard Heitzenrater has argued that this language sets up a sliding scale rather than an absolute standard for exercising judgment about the use of money. The four words that Heitzenrater points to as establishing this scale appear in Wesley's tenth sermon on the Sermon on the Mount: extremities, necessities, conveniences, and superfluities.[12]

This scale allowed all Methodists, whether rich or poor, to consider what they had to give. The language of extremities indicated not having enough for subsistence. Necessities meant having enough to survive, preferably of decent quality (enough nutritious food, proper clothing, adequate shelter). A few conveniences to make life easier were allowed. Having more than necessities and a few conveniences brought you to the level of superfluities, where the dangers to the soul and the danger of waste were a pressing problem.

Wesley expected Methodists to do all the good it was possible for them to do. While they were to do all they could without doing injury to the well-being of themselves or their dependents, this expectation did mean giving up some comfort and pleasure to help others. He expressed how this giving should work: "Let our superfluities give way to our neighbour's conveniences (and who then will have any superfluities left?); our conveniences to our neighbour's necessities; our necessities to his extremities."[13] No matter what your place on the economic scale, Wesley's scale for giving calls you to consider whether expenditures are necessary for carrying out your obligation to yourself or your dependents, or whether they can "give way" to someone else's need. This kind of reflection moves us from thinking about how to have more and allows us to recognize when we have enough.

As a guide for simpler living, this scale can be quite useful. It helps us to focus on how God has provided for what we need, and it helps us see how God can use us to provide for another's need. Regular attention to this kind of evaluation of our spending keeps us mindful of how our desires may be drawing us away from God and gives us an opportunity to refocus with a single eye on God. It can function to help us evaluate the way our lifestyle may be limiting our ability to help others. Opening our heart to "give way" to the need of another allows God's grace to work more powerfully in us.

Wesley never thought money was bad, and he wanted everyone to have enough to have a decent life. He knew the good it could do, but he also knew the temptation it brought to turn us away from God. The more resources we have, the less we think about the God who provided them. We begin to trust in ourselves and in our things more than we do in God. This is the fundamental danger of money. An intentionally simple life may not completely eliminate that danger, but making a conscious choice not to acquire more gives us a better chance to keep trusting in God. Seeking to increase riches sets us up to find our happiness in them instead of in God, and so we are misled into disloyalty that breaks relationship with God.

CONCLUDING THOUGHTS

Admittedly, there are economic differences between the twenty-first and the eighteenth centuries, and the details of Wesley's advice about money sometimes have to be adjusted to fit a different world. For instance, Wesley's recognition that we sometimes need to plan and save now has to be extended to planning and saving for the current social practice of retirement. On the other hand, the roots of middle class mass consumption of goods and entertainment were found even in Wesley's time, so his theological insight into the connection between money and happiness offers much wisdom relevant for today.

The link between money and happiness is complicated. Although economic security is a component of life satisfaction, happiness does not simply rise as income rises. Expectations may have more to do with happiness than increased financial resources do. We are happy (content or satisfied) when our expectations are met, but happiness may suffer if our expectations are out of line with the reality of our resources, no matter how high or low they may be. Expectations can be unreasonably inflated when we compare our lives to others who seem more successful, and happiness can suffer from those unmet expectations.

One of the ways Wesley's theology and practice works to help us find happiness in God is that it directs much of our effort to shaping good expectations.

The single eye that keeps our focus on God teaches us to desire God above all else instead of being distracted by other desires. Being attentive to when we might be tempted to serve mammon allows us to move our focus back to the only God who deserves our allegiance. Together with the expectation of being made perfect in love, the single eye keeps us looking for happiness in our relationship with God. Money does not and cannot satisfy this expectation. Clearly having this single expectation allows us to handle financial loss or financial gain with calmness and steadiness. There is freedom that comes from knowing that one's deepest well-being cannot be touched by the rise or fall of income.

Simple living does much to help us satisfy this expectation for happiness in God. Prioritizing what we need above what we want, and recognizing when we have enough, is a discipline that keeps us from trusting in something other than God. By keeping distractions of other desires to a minimum, it helps us keep focused on what really matters for the happiness we seek. It also allows us to use the resources that God provides for us in ways that express our love for God and for neighbor, and in doing so we actually gain the happiness we seek. Happiness in God is not tied to economic advantage, so spiritual well-being is available to anyone at any economic level.

One of the great barriers to happiness is the envy that happens when we compare our lives to others who have more than we do, but Wesley offers us a way to keep from falling into that trap. Instead of directing our attention to what others have that we do not, Wesley's sliding scale for evaluating the use of money directs our attention to how much we have and to how it may best be used. When we look at the lives of others, then, we are looking for their need and how we may use our resources to provide for that need. Cultivating this point of view rather than one that is always trying to "keep up" with others reverses our expectations and keeps us directed to finding happiness in God.

Much of Wesley's theology attempted to bring our desires and expectations to the surface for our reflection. He realized that this was where our spiritual lives were most vulnerable, so it was important to shape and direct ourselves to the desires and expectations that would lead us to what would make us truly and eternally happy, not only temporarily so.

Together with the expectation of being made perfect in love, the expectation of being fulfilled by a simple life focused on God provides us with a goal that is worthy of a follower of Jesus Christ. This is a goal that draws us forward to what will fulfill us as nothing else can—a fulfillment that is lasting and complete. When we allow God to shape our desires through a simple life with a single eye, we will stay on the way of salvation and gain the holiness and happiness to which that way leads.

ENDNOTES

1. John Wesley, Sermons 28 and 29, "Upon Our Lord's Sermon on the Mount," 8 and 9 in *The Sermons of John Wesley*, General Board of Global Ministries of The United Methodist Church, www.umcmission.org/Find-Resources/John-Wesley-Sermons/Sermon-28-Upon-Our-Lords-Sermon-on-the-Mount-8 and www.umcmission.org/Find-Resources/John-Wesley-Sermons/Sermon-29-Upon-Our-Lords-Sermon-on-the-Mount-9.

2. "Upon Our Lord's Sermon on the Mount 9," I.2–4.

3. Ibid., I.4–6.

4. John Wesley, Sermon 30, "Upon Our Lord's Sermon on the Mount 10," General Board of Global Ministries of The United Methodist Church, www.umcmission.org/Find-Resources/John-Wesley-Sermons/Sermon-30-Upon-Our-Lords-Sermon-on-the-Mount-10, 26.

5. John Wesley, "Upon Our Lord's Sermon on the Mount 9," 16.

6. John Wesley, Sermon 50, "The Use of Money," in *The Sermons of John Wesley*, General Board of Global Ministries of The United Methodist Church, www.umcmission.org/Find-Resources/John-Wesley-Sermons/Sermon-50-The-Use-of-Money.

7. John Wesley, Sermon 50, "The Use of Money," I.1–2, General Board of Global Ministries of The United Methodist Church, www.umcmission.org/Find-Resources/John-Wesley-Sermons/Sermon-50-The-Use-of-Money.

8. John Wesley, Sermon 88, "On Dress," in *The Sermons of John Wesley*, General Board of Global Ministries of The United Methodist Church, www.umcmission.org/Find-Resources/John-Wesley-Sermons/Sermon-88-On-Dress, 16.

9. John Wesley, "The Use of Money," III.5.

10. John Wesley, Sermon 87, "The Danger of Riches," in *The Sermons of John Wesley*, General Board of Global Ministries of The United Methodist Church, www.umcmission.org/Find-Resources/John-Wesley-Sermons/Sermon-87-The-Danger-of-Riches.

11. See www.umcmission.org/Find-Resources/John-Wesley-Sermons/ Sermon-126-On-the-Danger-of-Increasing-Riches.

12. Richard Heitzenrater, *The Poor and the People Called Methodists* (Nashville: Kingswood Books, 2002), 28–35.

13. John Wesley, Sermon 30, "Upon Our Lord's Sermon on the Mount, 10," in *The Sermons of John Wesley*, General Board of Global Ministries of The United Methodist Church, www.umcmission.org/Find-Resources/John-Wesley-Sermons/Sermon-30-Upon-Our-Lords-Sermon-on-the-Mount-10, 26.

Epilogue

John Wesley summed up authentic Christian faith as gratitude and benevolence. The gratitude that we show to God for saving and providing for us personally leads directly to wishing well for our fellow creatures. When our hearts are filled with thankfulness to God and generosity to others, then we have gained the holiness of heart that God wants for us. When we are thus renewed in the image of God, we know the happiness for which we were made. He believed this was the message of the Bible: scriptural holiness and scriptural happiness.

If gratitude and benevolence sum up the "Happiness for which we were made,"[1] and if they lead to the happiness for which we were made, then we learn something important about how to gain scriptural happiness. A thankful heart is a happy heart, so the things we do to remember what God has done for us (reading scripture, praying, singing) contribute to our happiness by making us more thankful. A happy heart is one that lives for others, so the works God has given us to do for our neighbor also contribute to our happiness by making us more generous and helpful. A heart that is thankful to God and that lives for others will be truly content.

Wesley knew that many Christians in his time never truly knew this happiness, and so he saw his ministry as calling them to this possibility that they were missing. For many today, happiness may not seem like a noble goal for Christians, and it is true that, happiness without holiness is superficial and fleeting. On the other hand, holiness without happiness is a burden that may seem pointless. Our heritage shows us how to hold the two together so we may be the people God calls us to be and know the deep and lasting happiness that God intends for us.

ENDNOTES

1. John Wesley, Sermon 114, "The Unity of the Divine Being," www.umcmission.org/Find-Resources/John-Wesley-Sermons/Sermon-114-The-Unity-of-the-Divine-Being, 17.

Selected Bibliography

Popular music, some pop-culture references, author interviews, and dictionary references are excluded from this list of works cited.

Alexander, Ruth. "Where Are You on the Global Pay Scale?" *BBC News Magazine*. March 29, 2012.

Alkon, Cheryl. "Money: Go With the Flow." *USA Weekend*. July 12–14, 2013.

Amagada, Joseph. "Definition of Happiness: What Is Happiness?" Ezinearticles.com. March 10, 2009. http://ezinearticles.com/?Definition-of-Happiness—What-is-Happiness?&id=2050358.

Ban Breathnach, Sarah. *Simple Abundance: A Daybook of Comfort and Joy*. New York: Warner Books, Inc., 1995.

Bruzzese, Anita. "On the Job: What Is the Formula for Happiness?" *USA Today*. September 1, 2013.

Center for Disease Control and Prevention. "National Marriage and Divorce Rate Trends," National Vital Statistics System. February 19, 2013. www.cdc.gov/nchs/nvss/marriage_divorce_tables.htm.

Charry, Ellen T. *God and the Art of Happiness*. Grand Rapids, Mich: William B. Eerdmans Publishing Company, 2010.

Chilcote, Paul Wesley. *Her Own Story: Autobiographical Portraits of Early Methodist Women*. Nashville: Kingswood Books, 2001.

Coca-Cola Advertisting Television Home Page. "The 'Hilltop' Ad: The Story of a Commercial." Accessed September 14, 2014. http://memory. loc.gov/ammem/ccmphtml/colaadv.html.

Copen, Casey E., Kimberly Daniels, et al., "First Marriages in the United States: Data From the 2006–2010 National Survey of Family Growth," National Health Statistics Reports, No. 49, March 22, 2012. www.cdc. gov/nchs/data/nhsr/nhsr049.pdf.

Dale, Steve. "How Dogs Spread Happiness." *USA Today*, January 24, 2012, http://usatoday30.usatoday.com/news/health/wellness/pets/story/ 2012-01-24/How-dogs-spread-happiness/52756792/1.

Diener, Ed. "What is happiness?" *This Emotional Life*. PBS, 2011. www.pbs.org/thisemotionallife/topic/happiness/what-happiness.

Fore, William F. *Mythmakers: Gospel, Culture and the Media*. New York: Friendship Press, 1990.

Foster, Rick and Greg Hicks. *How We Choose to Be Happy: The 9 Choices of Extremely Happy People—Their Secrets, Their Stories*. New York: G.P Putnam's Sons, 1999.

Hamilton, James and John Tylee. "Ten ads that changed advertising." *Campaign*, May 18, 2007, www.campaignlive.co.uk/news/658586.

Heitzenrater, Richard. *The Poor and the People Called Methodists*. Nashville: Kingswood Books, 2002.

Hoffman, Elisha A. "Is Your All on the Altar?" 1900. Public Domain.

Howell, Ryan T. "How Much Does Happiness Cost? Not Much."
   Psychology Today. April 21, 2012. www.psychologytoday.com/blog/
   cant-buy-happiness/201204/how-much-does-happiness-cost-not-much.

Jones, Serene. "Selling Social Justice Short." *Time.* February 14, 2014,
   http://time.com/7359/selling-social-justice-short.

Kahneman, Daniel and Angus Deaton. "High income improves evaluation
   of life but not emotional well-being," Proceedings of the National
   Academy of Sciences of the United States of America. August 4, 2010.
   www.pnas.org/content/107/38/16489.

Kilbourne, Jean. *Killing Us Softly 3, Advertising's Image of Women.*
   Northhampton, MA: Media Education Foundation, 2000.

Kluger, Jeffrey, "The Happiness of Pursuit." *Time*, July 8, 2013. http://
   content.time.com/time/magazine/article/0,9171,2146449,00.html

Linder, Melanie. "What People Are Still Willing to Pay For." *Forbes*, January
   15, 2009. www.forbes.com/2009/01/15/self-help-industry-ent-sales-
   cx_ml_0115selfhelp.html.

"Longest-Married Couple: 83-Year Marriage Ends After Wife's Death."
   Huffington Post. Updated April 12, 2013. http://www.huffingtonpost.
   com/2013/04/11/longest-married-couple_n_3062396.html.

Marist College Institute for Public Opinion. "Generation to Generation:
   Money Matters." August 13, 2013. http://maristpoll.marist.edu/
   wp-content/misc/Home%20instead/Money%20Matters_
   April%202012_FINAL.pdf.

Miller, Vincent J. *Consuming Religion: Christian Faith and Practice in a Consumer Culture*. New York: Continuum, 2004.

Mohney, Nell W. *Just Choose Happiness: A Guide to Joyous Living*. Nashville: Abingdon Press, 2009.

Moore, Thomas. "Come Ye Disconsolate." *Sacred Songs*. 1816. Revised 1824.

Murlin, John. "The Life of John Murlin." Vol. 2 in *The Lives of Early Methodist Preachers, Chiefly Written by Themselves*, edited by Thomas Jackson. London: John Mason, 1837.

Owens, Deborah and Brenda Lane Rixhardson. *A Purse of Your Own: An Easy Guide to Financial Security*. New York: Touchstone, 2009.

Parents Television Council. "Facts and TV Statistics." Accessed September 18, 2014. w2.parentstv.org/main/research/facts.aspx

Pfeiffer, Eric. "Nebraska couple wear matching outfits every day for 35 years." *Yahoo! News*, May 29, 2012. http://news.yahoo.com/blogs/sideshow/nebraska-cou.

Powell, John. *Happiness is an Inside Job*. Allen, Texas: Tabor Publishing, 1989.

Prince William, interview by Max Foster, CNN, August 19, 2013, www.cnn.com/2013/08/19/world/prince-william-transcript.

Reilly, Lucas "By the Numbers: How Americans Spend Their Money." Mental_Floss. July 17, 2012, http://mentalfloss.com/article/31222/numbers-how-americans-spend-their-money.

Savacool, Julia "Find the silver lining in hard times," *USA Weekend*, November 9–11, 2012.

Shoemaker, Pamela J. and Stephen D. Reese. *Mediating the Message, Theories of Influences on Mass Media Content*. New York: Longman, 1991.

Smith, Roff. "Five Takeaways from the UN's Global Report on Happiness." *National Geographic*, September 9, 2013.

The Book of Resolutions of The United Methodist Church 2012. Nashville: United Methodist Publishing House, 2013.

The United Methodist Hymnal, Nashville: Abingdon Press, 1989.

UNESCO. "World Water Day 2013: International Year of Water Cooperation." Accessed September 18, 2914. www.unwater.org/water-cooperation-2013/water-cooperation/facts-and-figures/en.

United Nations Sustainable Development Solutions Network. "World Happiness Report 2013." Edited by John Helliwell, Richard Layard, Jeffrey Sachs. http://www.earth.columbia.edu/sitefiles/file/Sachs%20Writing/2012/World%20Happiness%20Report.pdf.

Vickhoff, Björn and Helge Malmgren, et al. "Music Structure Determines Heart Rate Variability of Singers." *Frontiers in Psychology* 4, July 2013.

Wesley, Charles. *Hymns and Sacred Poems*, 1739. Accessed September 18, 2014. http://divinity.duke.edu/sites/default/files/documents/cswt/01_Hymns_and_Sacred_Poems_%281739%29_CW_Verse_mod.pdf.

Wesley, John. "John Wesley Sermons," *The Sermons of John Wesley*, General Board of Global Ministries of The United Methodist Church. Accessed September 18, 2014. www.umcmission.org/Find-Resources/John-Wesley-Sermons.

Wesley, John. "Reasons Against a Separation from the Church of England," *The Methodist Societies: History, Nature, and Design.* Edited by Rupert E. Davies. *The Works of John Wesley: The Bicentennial Edition,* vol. 9. Edited by Frank Baker. Nashville: Abingdon Press, 1984ff.

Wesley, John. *Journals and Diaries I.* Edited by W. Reginald Ward and Richard P. Heitzenrater. *The Works of John Wesley: The Bicentennial Edition,* vol. 18. Edited by Frank Baker. Nashville: Abingdon Press, 1984ff.

Wesley, John. *Journals and Diaries II.* Edited by W. Reginald Ward and Richard P. Heitzenrater. *The Works of John Wesley: The Bicentennial Edition,* vol. 19. Edited by Frank Baker. Nashville: Abingdon Press, 1984ff.

World Council of Churches. Commission on World Mission and Evangelism. "Together Towards Life: Mission and Evangelism in Changing Landscapes." Edited by Joosep Keum. Geneva: WCC Publications, 2013.

Wuorio, Jeff. "I'll Take That, and That, and That." *USA Weekend.* July 12–14, 2013.

CREATED FOR HAPPINESS:
UNDERSTANDING YOUR LIFE IN GOD

Participant's Guide

Cynthia A. Bond Hopson

INTRODUCTION

On Happiness and Such

What is happiness and why does it matter? Asking those two questions may seem crass and irrelevant since most of us expect to be happy in our lives and activities. We invest at least some thought and effort into what would be required to arrive at a place called happiness and spend some time there, yet few of us have dissected the concept or even considered it worthy of study.

In many cultures, simple lives are eked out on fragile mountainsides and in ravaged valleys where what it takes to be happy is clearly not defined by things like automobiles, lavish feasts, or expendable incomes. Rather, in these instances, family, friends, and peace are treasured and living is not so much thriving as it is surviving. In more developed nations and cultures, extravagant and conspicuous consumption fueled by greed, status seeking, and the accumulation of those very things that separate the haves from the have-nots may be present, but true happiness may still be elusive.

So, as we begin an in-depth examination of the pursuit of happiness, be prepared for a rich, robust, and passionate conversation that may be uncomfortable at times but will ultimately enrich all those who participate. Perhaps you have chosen this study because you want to get a deeper, more meaningful understanding of how happiness affects the quality of your life or perhaps you have chosen it because it sounded like fun. Maybe it's even a little bit of both—whatever the case, let's covenant to come with open minds and an intention to learn new ways to look at and enrich the gifts God so generously gives us to make our lives worth living. Like with anything, the more you put into it, the more you will receive.

As you prepare for this time of study, ask God for grace and courage so you may experience all that this study has to offer. May you be blessed and enriched as we begin this journey together.

PREPARING FOR THIS STUDY

You have arrived at Mission u. You've greeted longtime friends, made some new ones, gotten settled in the room, now what? Begin thinking about your hopes and dreams for this time—what will happiness look like? Happiness is a personal experience so what it looks like for you may be very different from what it looks like for your peers. Also, begin thinking about your commitment to be fully engaged. You will do your readings and discussions in groups during class, but to get the most from the four two-hour sessions, consider reading on your own so you may get a deeper sense of how happiness, or the lack of it, affects you and how you live your life.

The goals of this study include:

- Defining happiness in the sacred and secular spaces so you will know it when you see it;
- Examining what the Bible has to say about happiness;
- Gaining a better understanding of the ways happiness affects us and the choices we ultimately make;
- Linking John Wesley's philosophy of happiness, wholeness, and holiness to how we choose happiness in today's society; and finally
- Examining if a simpler pursuit may lead us to the conclusion we desire.

The Participant's Guide is divided into four sessions that will cover the seven chapters of *Created for Happiness: Understanding your Life in God*. The text that has been carefully and lovingly prepared for this study examines happiness from many angles—pop cultural depictions, how Methodism founder John Wesley's social holiness gets lived out, probing inquiry into how self-image is formed, and the role of happiness in the scriptures. The study aims to make your time challenging yet satisfying, interesting and mind expanding, refreshing but a little uncomfortable.

How do I prepare for this study?
About two weeks before your class starts, begin preparing through the following activities:

- Begin a time of deliberate prayer to get centered.
- Keep a diary or journal.
- Spend at least ten minutes every day observing people as they go about their daily lives. In your diary, make a section with the following headings: gender, approximate age, setting, what prompted the response/behavior (i.e., seeing a cute baby on the plane made half the passengers stop and engage). This should be done discreetly and informally (without staring, please) during the course of your day.
- Watch the following movies about happiness:
  o *Secondhand Lions*,
  o *The Pursuit of Happyness*, and
  o *With Honors*.
- Begin reading the text.

CREATING A CLIMATE FOR LEARNING

When everyone shares thoughts and opinions, we all learn more. Participants who attend Mission u come in all shapes, sizes, and emotional stages. While you have come to be challenged and informed, please be gracious and prepared to make sure each person has an opportunity to have a say if they'd like.

Establish a posture for learning and reflection by planning some quiet time for discernment and contemplation. Remember to bring your Bible and a notebook to every session.

CONFIDENTIALITY AND RULES OF ENGAGEMENT

"What happens in Vegas, stays in Vegas," isn't just a slogan—it is a poignant reminder that some things we see and experience need to be kept between God and us!

Establishing this understanding as the class code will be important. During your opening session, your instructor will work purposefully to create a safe and sacred space for you to learn, grow, and share your feelings. There may be several people from your church in your class. If this makes you uncomfortable, you might want to look for other sessions of this class where possible. While there is no way to assure complete confidentiality, this expectation will be expressed early and often.

A code of conduct similar to the one below will help govern your time together to ensure every person is seen, heard, respected, and valued. The class will read the rules aloud to stress the importance of adherence. Is anything missing from the code below? If it will add to the atmosphere of better understanding, please share it with your instructor.

Sample code of conduct
- I will pay attention and listen carefully to what is being said both verbally and nonverbally without jumping to conclusions.
- I will refrain from using electronic devices that might distract me from the discussion.
- I will not interrupt others when they speak.

- I will remember to be kind, sensitive, and empathetic.
- I will try to put myself in the other person's shoes before I judge.
- I know there is always more for me to learn.
- I will work to understand and to be understood.
- I know we are all entitled to our opinions. The world will not end if the speakers don't share mine.
- If I disagree, I will not pout, sulk, or be disagreeable.
- I will try to avoid arguments around politics and religion.
- I will not be rude or dismissive.
- I will respect my class, do my assignments, and arrive on time.
- I will not share what goes on in this class with outsiders.
- I understand that cultural differences may make others reluctant to speak quickly and loudly—I will refrain from responding to every comment to allow time for contemplation and discernment.
- I will pray that this class will bless and enrich each of us.

SCRIPTURES

The following scriptures have been selected to coordinate with this study:

Deuteronomy 30:15–20
Deuteronomy 6:4–15
Nehemiah 8:9–10
Psalm 32:11
Psalm 35:9
Psalm 37:1–9
Psalm 105:43
Psalm 112
Psalm 121
Psalm 126:5
Psalm 119:1–16; 33–40; 73–80
Psalm 144:15
Proverbs 3:13

Proverbs 6:20
Matthew 5:1–14
Matthew 6:19–21
Matthew 6:25–34
Matthew 22:34–40
Matthew 25:31–46
John 15:11
Philippians 4:4–7
Philippians 4:8–13
2 Timothy 1–7
3 John 1:2–4
Revelation 21:1–7

DEFINING AND CREATING HAPPINESS IN OUR SACRED AND SECULAR SPACES (CHAPTERS 1 AND 2)

"A cheerful heart is a good medicine . . ."

—Proverbs 17:22a

SESSION OBJECTIVES

- Explore happiness as a tangible concept.
- Define and better understand how happiness is created, defined, and manufactured by media in the secular arenas.
- See how and if secular influences create a culture of want or unrealistic expectations.
- Eliminate barriers to wholesome happiness.
- Discuss the distinction between happiness and joy.

OPENING WORSHIP

Scripture
Deuteronomy 30:15–20; Matthew 6:25–34

Opening prayer (unison)
Lord, we have come to this place from near and far, from our chaotic lives

and rusty, dusty routines, from all that was and is to all that might be, to the possibilities. We welcome you to our midst and ask that you be near us and breathe your gentle mercies on us so we may leave this place renewed. Amen.

Questions for reflection
What does Deuteronomy 30:15–30 invite us to do?

Matthew 6:26–27 reminds us to stop worrying because God supplies our earthly needs of food and clothing. What are some of the other tangible and intangible things that make life meaningful?

God feeds the sparrows and you are worth more than that—how much are you worth to God's kingdom? Are there things you can do to increase your worth to God?

What are some of the things you mentioned here that belong in the worship center to symbolize your Godward journey?

THE CODE OR GROUND RULES

Read the rules under "Confidentiality and Rules of Engagement" in the Introduction and see if there are ones you want to delete or add. The Sample Code will be posted on the wall.

QUESTIONS FOR REFLECTION

Discuss the following questions at your table. Select a note taker/reporter for your group.

- What is it about this image of happiness that makes people want to buy this product or experience?
- What are your favorite advertisements for cars, trucks, deodorant, hair and skin care. Why are they your favorites?

- What are the feelings and emotions that the images in the advertisements evoke in you?
- How does the media industry use images, colors, sounds, and other means to package happiness?
- Come up with one question that you would like to ask the makers or advertisers of products that promote happiness.

Share your insights with the whole group.

The leader will invite one person from each table to collect all the consumerist images and products of happiness to bring to the worship center, and place them at the altar of consumerist culture or *mammon*.

TIME WITH THE TEXT

In small groups discuss the following questions based on your reading of Chapters 1 and 2.

1. What are the things that make for true happiness according to Cynthia Bond Hopson?
2. What are some of the definitions that she included to describe happiness?
3. What would you like to add to the definitions?
4. In your small groups, write down your insights and definitions on your index cards.

START WITH ME, GOD: LET'S SEE WHAT'S INSIDE

William F. Fore, a United Methodist minister who wrote the mission study *Mythmakers: Gospel, Culture and the Media*, explains, "If I could ask a fish, 'How do you like the water?' the answer probably would be, 'What water?' It's hard to analyze what you take for granted. If your leader asks you, 'How do you like the media environment?' would your response be, 'What media environment?' Media supply the mental environment in which we 'swim' every day. Newspapers, books, films, radio, and television are called media because they mediate to us the things that lie outside our direct personal experience. They are the bridges between our environment and us. Media create the world in our minds."[1]

We want to be happy, but may not realize or understand what's subconsciously blocking our progress. It may be that we are caught in the consumerist culture that shapes our lives in such a way that ours becomes a life in a media fishbowl.

It may be that childhood wounds and scars or low self-esteem block our Godward journey. Whatever it is, we need to address it and move forward triumphantly. Legendary novelist and Harlem Renaissance giant James Baldwin's philosophy was that addressing issues may not fix them, but they certainly can't be fixed unless they are confronted. Today, let's see if we can name our fears, all those things that distort true happiness, and resolve to confront them at their source.

ACTIVITY 1: TAKE THE HAPPINESS SURVEY

After completing the survey found in Appendix A, use the following quesitons in your discussion:

- What surprised you most?
- What is one thing you would like to change?
- What is your biblical concept of happiness and joy?

ACTIVITY 2: TAKING OUT THE GARBAGE!

Sit quietly and think about what makes you happy, and what your vision of happiness is. On index cards, write the words "To Keep" on top and list all the things that come to mind. Celebrate the things on this list.

Now, what are things that block or get in the way of happiness? Use more index cards or slips of paper to write all the things that make you sad or unhappy: addictions, molestation, estrangement, unhappy marriages, bad credit. Write freely, nobody will see these things that will go in the garbage can—it's garbage, remember? It is cathartic to name the things that bog us down, so bring all this "trash" to the garbage individually and repeat this affirmation:

Lord, today we have taken out the trash and now we're free to be all you have created us to be. Amen.

CLOSING WORSHIP

The leaders of the small groups will gather your "To Keep" index cards and place them at the altar. Join hands for the closing litany and prayer.

Closing litany

Leader: Today, we choose happiness and we intend to move forward and count it all as joy because you have said that is your plan for us!

People: **Lord, today we are free to be.**

Leader: Yes, Lord, we are free to be triumphant, we are free to be at peace, we have given you our scars, our troubles, our miseries, our doubts, and fears—all the things that distract us.

People: **Lord, today we are free. Hallelujah!**

Leader: And whom the Son sets free is free indeed.

ALL: **Praise the Lord. Amen**

ASSIGNMENT FOR THE NEXT SESSION

- Read Chapters 3 and 4.
- Individual activity: Visualize a journey. Draw a picture of a journey on a piece of construction paper or in your notebook. It can be a road, a trail, footsteps, a boat, or a ship on the sea. What are the

things that are most essential for you to journey toward becoming a citizen of the household of God?

- What does it take to be the change that you want to see? Name these changes.
- What are some of the things that sidetrack you from this journey? Who or which small group can you rely on to keep you on the right track?

ENDNOTES

1. William F. Fore, "Swimming in the Media Fishbowl," **response**, July 2004, 10.

WHAT THE "GOOD BOOK" SAYS ABOUT BEING HAPPY

(CHAPTERS 3 AND 4)

"By talking to yourself every hour of the day, you can direct yourself to think thoughts of courage and happiness, thoughts of power and peace. By talking to yourself about the things you have to be grateful for, you can fill your mind with thoughts that soar and sing."

—Dale Carnegie [1]

SESSION OBJECTIVES

- Look at media influence on concepts of happiness and acceptability.
- Examine how our self-images are shaped.
- Affirm our positive attributes and self-worth.
- Encourage participants to begin thinking more critically about what they expose themselves to and what they know, feel, and understand about themselves and their emotional well-being.
- Explore the biblical understandings of happiness.

OPENING WORSHIP

Scripture
Quietly meditate on James 1:2.
Read Matthew 5: 1–11 aloud substituting the word "happy" for "blessed."

Opening litany and reflection

Right: My joy comes from knowing I am a child of God.
I was not promised nor do I expect an easy life.
I was promised that my Savior would never leave me so . . .

Left: I walk with confidence knowing I am never alone.
I delight in the glorious kingdom created for me
I anticipate sun and rain, some sweet days and some bitter.
That is life.

Right: I am on an exciting journey
With God and God's people.
I am in love with all creation.

Left: Tomorrow may knock me down,
But I will rise.
Not on my own power.
No, not with my own feeble might.

Right: But with the power Peter and John
gave the lame man at the Beautiful Gate;
with the faith of Shadrach,
Meshach and Abednego;
with the confidence of David
over his foe Goliath;

Left: with Mary, Martha, Mary Magdalene, Salome, Joanna, Susanna and
many others who journeyed with Jesus supporting his risk-taking mission.

All: For with God, I am mighty,
Equipped for the journey ahead, clothed in righteousness,
and strong.
(Written by Roger A. Hopson for this study. Used with permission.)

DEBRIEFING AND REFLECTION

After you finish the litany, take time to debrief from the previous session with the following questions:

1. What was the most important thing you heard?
2. What did you discover about yourself from your homework assignment?
3. What does happiness look like?

TIME WITH THE TEXT

- What are the key themes in Chapter 3?
- How do images of media shape our desires, longings, and self-image?
- Is the culture of the church powerful enough to counteract the constructed images of happiness in the media? Why? Why not?
- What are some of the actions that we can take to educate people to be critical viewers of media and advertisements?

Small group discussion

Let us invite ourselves into the sites of happiness in the biblical landscape. In four groups, examine one of the following themes: Happiness in the Law, Happiness in the Psalms, Happiness in the Gospels, and Happiness in Paul's Epistles, and summarize the key concepts in them by answering the following questions:

Each group should select a note taker/reporter for their discussion.

1. What is your understanding of happiness from these Bible readings?
2. How is happiness both inner-directed as well as other-directed?

3. Which biblical understanding from these readings can enrich your spiritual journey?
4. Which one seems hard to follow?
5. What are some of the ways you cope when happy days seem far away?
6. Sarah Lancaster says in Chapter 4:

> The practice of distinguishing "happiness" from "joy," arose in order to do something important, that is to distinguish true happiness from false happiness. But to use the word "happiness" only for false happiness is misleading when we read translations of the Bible or theologians like John Wesley who use "happy" and "happiness" quite freely when they talk about life with God. In fact, because some English translations of the Bible do use the word "happy" at all, we must think about what is meant by that word.

What is the key concept in this argument? Why is it important to reclaim the usage of the word "happiness" in its wholesome meaning for one's individual and collective spiritual journey?
7. Where have you seen God at work in your life, church, and community?

START WITH ME GOD: LET'S SEE WHAT'S INSIDE

Participate in individual reflection and journaling on things and relationships that make up the word happiness.

1. What are some of the ways I can cope when happy days seem far away?
2. What are some of the ways God blesses those who faithfully follow?

3. How can we be more effective in sharing our faith?
4. What role do those who are poor play in a discussion about what God expects from us?
5. What more can you do to be faithful and obedient to hear and answer God's call on your life?
6. What are some of the things we can do to please God?
7. Does global warming have a place in a discussion about happiness and keeping God's commands?
8. How do we explain/reconcile death, destruction, and disaster with happiness, joy, and trust in God in a biblical context?

CLOSING WORSHIP: THINGS AND RELATIONSHIPS THAT MAKE UP THE WORD "HAPPINESS"

Prayer (unison)

God of life, we come before you this day. We are mindful of the things that please you. We are thankful for the community of faith and we cherish the relationships that help us realize your mission of happiness on earth. Amen.

Closing litany (unison)

Leader: God is love and is always there to care for and about me. He gave his very best to prove it. How do I know?

People: The Bible tells me so.

Leader: God can do anything and everything. Really cool stuff like putting out fires in furnaces, getting rid of mean ol' giants, you name it, and my God can do it. How do I know?

People: The Bible tells me so.

Leader: Our God is mighty. He reigns with wisdom, power, and grace. How do I know?

People: The Bible tells me so.

Leader: So, I am not afraid of anything because God is always with me. How do I know?

ALL: For the Bible tells us so. Hallelujah!

Closing prayer (unison)
Lord, peace and happiness are yours to give and ours to graciously receive. We thank you. We thank you for our families, for our friends, for food and shelter, all the sources of joy you bless us with daily. Remind us Lord to share your joy and your peace with all those we meet. Let the world see you at work in our lives—enrich them for your glory. Amen.

ASSIGNMENT FOR THE NEXT SESSION

- Read Chapters 5 and 6.
- Read your favorite happiness scriptures, or those you rely on for strength and courage.
- Journal about two times when these passages have made the difference between despair and hope.
- Complete these statements: If I had a coat of arms, it would look like_____*(fill in the blank using words and/or an image).* The crest representing my core of happiness would look like _____ *(fill in the blank; optional: draw a coat of arms or create one from construction paper).*

ENDNOTES

1. Dale Carnegie, *How to Stop Worrying and Start Living*, 1948.

JOHN WESLEY AND THE METHODISTS

(CHAPTERS 5 AND 6)

"Let your words be the genuine picture of your heart."

—John Wesley

SESSION OBJECTIVES

- Examine further biblical references of happiness.
- Examine John Wesley's views on happiness in detail.
- Grapple with Wesley's understandings of happiness and their modern-day relevance.
- Understand the power of lifestyle choices and how they affect decisions and outcomes.

OPENING WORSHIP

Opening prayer (in unison)
O Lord, our Lord, we come now to witness to your love and grace. We thank you for happiness, joy, peace, contentment, and all these words represent in our dailiness. They are good and perfect gifts from you and we graciously receive them. Amen.

DEBRIEFING AND REFLECTION

From your homework, share scripture passages that made a difference in your life.

Share your word-pictures of your coat of arms. What is the happiness crest on your coat of arms or what is the core of happiness for you?

TIME WITH THE TEXT

John Wesley's influence more than two hundred thirty years after the denomination's founding is amazing and significant. Work in small groups to learn more about him.

- Group 1: Read the sections titled "The Image of God" and "Salvation and Happiness" in Chapter 5, and dramatize the impact of the findings and include how they affected your preconceived notions of happiness.

- Group 2: Read the sections titled "Happiness through Holiness," "Happiness as a Feeling," and "Heaviness." Share stories of a mentor or role model who has embodied happiness in the midst of it all, including heaviness and sorrow. Write their names on index cards.

- Group 3: Read the section titled "Singing" in Chapter 6. Also, look at the various hymns of John and Charles Wesley, and discuss the images they use for joy and happiness to see if they are still relevant today. Be sure to look at "O for a Thousand Tongues to Sing" and "Love Divine, All Loves Excelling."

Cultural diversity and living out biblical and Wesleyan understanding of happiness

Discuss the following questions with the whole group:

- What are some understandings of happiness from different ethnic and racial groups?
- How is the "image of God" interpreted and appropriated in different cultures and categories of people (race, ethnicity, gender, class, etc.)?
- Is John Wesley a role model?
- Are you a role model? Why or why not?

CLOSING WORSHIP

Celebrate the work you have done so far in this and the other two sessions. Where are you now versus where you were two sessions ago? Plan to share at least one thing you've learned.

Closing litany

Leader: We rejoice today for your servant John Wesley and we thank you for his life and ministry. You have created each of us with a grand plan for our lives, too.

People: **Lord, we are ready to live into your will for us. Help us to seek your will.**

ALL: **Lord, we come today with our hearts and hands open. We want to become a vessel you can use. Warm our hearts and send us forth to be your people in the world's parishes. We want to be the yeast that brings about change, silently and steadily for the good in our communities, so all may taste and see that the Lord is good, always good. Amen.**

ASSIGNMENT FOR THE NEXT SESSION

- Read Chapter 7 and the Epilogue.
- Be prepared to sit according to your conferences, districts, or clusters, as the case may be, and work on action plans in the next session. Come with action plans that can be implemented individually and collectively. Your ideas for action should include ways of adopting voluntary simplicity, addressing consumerist culture promoted by media, and implementing spiritual practices for the formation of God-intended happiness as seen in the Bible and Wesleyan understandings.

SESSION 4

LOOKING IN THE RIGHT PLACES?
(CHAPTER 7 AND EPILOGUE)

"I think happiness is what makes you pretty. Period. Happy people are beautiful. They become like a mirror and reflect that happiness."

—Drew Barrymore

SESSION OBJECTIVES

- Look at ways of addressing media's promotions of a consumerist culture, especially concepts and images of happiness and acceptability.
- Affirm positive use of media and information technologies.
- Commit ourselves to the spiritual practices that help embody happiness as outlined in the Bible.
- Select practices from John Wesley that are useful for us to be a witnessing faith community in today's world.
- Create actions plans to undertake voluntary simplicity.

OPENING WORSHIP

Sit according to your annual conference, district, or cluster of local churches.

How can you work individually and collectively to be the church in the world?

TIME WITH THE TEXT

In small groups discuss:

- What are the key themes in Chapter 7 and the Epilogue?
- Pick *one* key phrase that is significant for your journey from being a mere consumer of products to becoming a citizen in the household of God.
- What are some of the things you could do to simplify your life and increase your chances of happiness?

SHARING ACTION PLANS

The following are some options to work on in your group and at home. (Some of these are taken from "Action Ideas" in the July 2004 issue of **response**, p. 29.)

1. Develop the habit of critically analyzing your media usage.
2. Outline steps to make media more accountable to the needs and interests of the public.
3. Spend more time community building.
4. Use social media to promote social justice issues and to make a better world for all people.
5. Support community radio. Hundreds of small stations need program content and moral and economic support. Send them copies of newsletters, event announcements, and study topics. Support station fund drives with volunteerism.
6. Send information to community, ethnic, and alternative-language newspapers and other media channels. Your local church, conference, and United Methodist Women members are taking a stance on care for the earth, peace, and other social justice issues. Be guests in the program.

7. Join community networks. Neighborhoods are connected through the Internet with community bulletin boards that invite people to events and public hearings.
8. Be advocates for community media.
9. Organize a spiritual growth study on *Created for Happiness* in your local church.
10. Take concrete steps to practice happiness as outlined in the Bible.
11. Make efforts to reclaim the word "happiness," which the consumerist culture has appropriated. Use the H-word (happiness) more often as part of your spiritual vocabulary.
12. Begin to voluntarily lead a life of simplicity.
13. Participate in self-care.
14. Seek other-directed actions (participating in your community, visiting nursing homes, participating in advocacy efforts, etc.)

PLANNING THE STEPS AS A GROUP

Come up with some definite action ideas (including ideas to study this text and address consumerist culture) to be implemented as a group. Develop some steps to implement them. Determine the following:

- The time frame when this should take place,
- Groups within the church that you can partner with,
- Secular organizations in your area that are engaged in addressing the same issue, and
- Next steps.

SHARING

Each group shares the action ideas they have developed and the steps to implement them.

INDIVIDUAL WORK

Answer this statement: When I get home, I will _____
_____ .

(See the examples below, but what you decide to do is up to you.)

- Enjoy life more by doing the things I love.
- Share my joy by volunteering for a worthy cause. (These could include food banks, literacy councils and GED preparation for prisoners, family shelters, humane societies, Meals on Wheels.)
- Analyze what I'm doing with my time so I won't take on anything new unless I'm letting something else go.
- I will focus this year on the quality of my activities rather than the quantity. Anything that I don't have to do and that I'm not enjoying, I will give up so I can take on something I do enjoy.
- Tackle that stubborn project I've been avoiding.
- Read at least three bestsellers in the next year.
- Keep my "Happiness Journal" going as a gentle reminder that I am blessed and as an opportunity to spend time with God.
- Eat healthier foods and exercise at least four hours a week.
- I will make myself a bucket list—those things I want to do before I kick the bucket (die) and I'll get busy completing it.
- Learn a new language.
- Rest when I'm tired.

Steps to achieve the individual goals I have set
- Determine the time frame.
- Ask what financial commitment might be involved.
- Develop concrete steps to accomplishing each goal.

CLOSING WORSHIP

Take ten minutes to reflect and debrief. Ask yourself:

1. How have your thoughts and understanding about happiness and joy changed?
2. What are the action ideas that you have decided to implement individually?
3. Take time to pause and reflect on how you are going to be part of the collective action/ideas your group has already shared.

Closing litany (unison)
Wind Beneath My Wings

I have been given this day to savor or waste.
I can scurry with the driven or set my own pace.
I can dance with the children
Before they learn to fly,
Or live in isolation, never asking why.
I can live for others and claim my place in the sun,
Or I can whither alone, seeking and loving none.
The choices I make today will echo through my soul
Will I be a shadow or will I be whole?
(Written by Roger A. Hopson for this study. Used with permission.)

Closing prayer
Our God and Creator, we belong to you, heart, mind, body, and spirit. You shower us with patience and mercy and for that we are grateful. Remind us, Lord, that your plan is for us to be happy and whole and we will seek your will in being so. We will go now in peace. Amen.

Happiness Survey

Take your time and think carefully about your answers. You will be asked to share some of your answers with the class, but this information is to help you better understand happiness in its intricacies.

1. **What are seven things that make you smile whenever they are mentioned or come to mind?**

   1._____

   2._____

   3._____

   4._____

   5._____

   6._____

   7._____

2. **What are four things you are passionate about?**

   1._____

   2._____

   3._____

   4._____

3. What were you doing the last time you laughed so hard you cried?

_____

_____

_____

4. What are seven things you love about yourself?

1._____

2._____

3._____

4._____

5._____

6._____

7._____

5. Do you know how to give and receive compliments?

_____

_____

_____

_____

6. What do you need to change about how you honor yourself and your personal time?

_____

_____

_____

_____

7. Is there a difference between happiness and joyfulness for you? If so, which one are you now and what prompted it?

_____

_____

_____

_____

8. Do the people around you bring you down or lift you up? What do you do for the people around you?

_____

_____

_____

_____

9. What are four areas of your life where you could cultivate a greater sense of honesty and integrity?

1. _____

2. _____

3. _____

4. _____

10. Is there anybody you need to forgive? Do you need to be forgiven by someone else for something you've said or done? Can you let go and move on?

_____

_____

_____

11. Are you more than you have become?

_____

_____

_____

_____

12. When do you feel God's presence most in your life?

_____

_____

_____

_____

13. Are you a glass half-full or half-empty kind of person, or somewhere in between? What does "attitude is everything" mean to you?

_____

_____

_____

_____

14. This is what I did on the happiest day of my life:

_____

_____

_____

_____

APPENDIX B

Happiness Journal

Set aside at least ten minutes each day for the next thirty-one days to be on the lookout for happiness and use the following form to record your experience. Duplicate enough pages to use one a day for the month and keep them in a loose-leaf binder.

Today I am thankful for:

1. _____

2. _____

3. _____

4. _____

5. _____

6. _____

7. _____

8. _____

9. _____

10. _____

Here's how I can bring/share joy:

I will visit _____at the nursing home.

I will call/send a note to my _____ grade teacher/_____ profes-sor and tell her/him how they blessed me.

I will smile more today and say hello to two people I wouldn't ordinarily speak to: _____ and _____.

I will laugh loudly and often today.

I'm doing _____ today because it brings me unspeakable joy. Hallelujah!

About the Authors

Cynthia A. Bond Hopson is assistant general secretary of the Black College Fund and Ethnic Concerns at The United Methodist Church's General Board of Higher Education and Ministry in Nashville. In her work she interprets, promotes, and manages funding for the eleven United Methodist–related Historically Black Colleges and Universities. She received a B.A. in mass communications in 1985 from Clark College (now Clark Atlanta University); an M.S. in journalism from Murray (KY) State University in 1989; and a Ph.D. in journalism from Southern Illinois University in Carbondale in 2000. She is chief inspiration officer of Touched by Grace Ministry (www. touchedbygraceministry.com), an author, motivational speaker, and activist. She and her husband, Roger, a United Methodist minister, love to travel and spend time with their two children and four grandchildren.

Sarah Heaner Lancaster is Hazen G. Werner Professor of Theology at Methodist Theological School in Ohio. She received a B.A. from Rice University; M.Div. from Perkins School of Theology at Southern Methodist University; and Ph.D. from Southern Methodist University. She is the author of *The Pursuit of Happiness: Blessing and Fulfillment in Christian Faith* and *Women and the Authority of Scripture: A Narrative Approach*. She has been co-chair of the Wesleyan Studies Group of the American Academy of Religion and is currently a co-chair of the Oxford Institute of Methodist Theological Studies. She is an elder in the North Texas Conference of The United Methodist Church. She and her husband, Kermit, live in Westerville, Ohio.

Other Resources from United Methodist Women

Spanish translation of *Created for Happiness: Understanding Your Life in God*
by Cynthia A. Bond Hopson & Sarah Heaner Lancaster
ISBN: 978-1-940182-22-3
M3221
$10

Korean translation of *Created for Happiness: Understanding Your Life in God*
by Cynthia A. Bond Hopson & Sarah Heaner Lancaster
ISBN: 978-1-940182-23-0
M3222
$10

Articles on "Created for Happiness: Understanding Your Life in God" appear
in **response** magazine throughout the year.

Place your order with:
United Methodist Women Mission Resources
1-800-305-9857
www.umwmissionresources.org

Created for Happiness: Understanding Your Life in God webpage:
www.unitedmethodistwomen.org/happiness

Notes

Notes